INTRODUCTION

They say that, sometimes, our bodies pick up on things before our minds do.

In December 2015, I found myself sitting in a doctor's office, sobbing with frustration. It was my third appointment in as many months as we tried to find the source of some painful symptoms that had been impacting my life for almost a year. My doctor had run all of the usual tests, and some bonus ones to be thorough, but they hadn't found an obvious cause for my painful stomachaches, irritated skin, or foggy headaches.

I was glad, of course, that there wasn't a serious illness to worry about, but I also felt completely exasperated. Without a specific diagnosis, we were left with simply trying to treat the symptoms, something we'd had varying levels of success with over the previous months.

"We'll run some tests again in a couple of months' time," my doctor assured me. "And in the meantime, try to reduce your stress levels. Maybe give mindfulness a go."

I was flummoxed. My issues were with my physical health, not my mental health. And aside from these bewildering ailments, what did I have to be stressed about? Everything was going according to plan: my partner and I had recently gotten engaged and were about to buy our first home. Our social lives were thriving, and we were about to head off for a long weekend in Oslo, Norway, one of many European city trips we'd managed to squeeze in that year. And to top it all off, my career—the area of life that I'd always given the most focus and attention to—was thriving. I was working at the Walt Disney Company, an organisation famous for making people happy. My job afforded me incredible benefits, access to movie premieres, and, most importantly, respect and credibility whenever I answered the age-old question, "What do you do for a living?"

On paper, everything was perfect, and I'd worked hard to make it so. I was ticking off all of those societal achievements we're taught to strive for, and I felt sure that my "happily ever after" was waiting just around the corner. And yet, the doctor's words kept rolling around in my mind. Could my physical symptoms be caused by something going on in my mind? Could the choices I was making be taking their toll on my health?

Sophie Cliff

CHOOSE JOY

Relieve Burnout, Focus on Your Happiness, and
Infuse More Joy into Your Everyday Life

BLUE·STAR
PRESS

For Blossom,
who only ever knew joy

TABLE

OF

CONTENT

I started to notice some patterns. My stomachaches were always worse on Sunday evenings, as I anticipated my return to the office the next morning. The panic attacks I'd suffered since my teenage years were more frequent after falling into a comparison spiral, when I'd spend hours sizing up my life against my friends' or those of the people I followed on social media. My head would pound whenever I considered how busy my schedule was. I knew that my mind and body were connected, but still I was in denial.

Rather than interpreting these symptoms as a sign that something needed to change, I used it as an opportunity to beat myself up. I ignored the warning signs that my body was giving me, instead blanketing them in a cloud of guilt. I told myself that the problem lay with me: I had a lovely life, so why couldn't I just feel grateful and enjoy it?

At the time, I knew deep down that my life was lacking something, but I was too scared and uncertain to unpack what that thing might have been. Now, after years of soul-searching and research, I see it so clearly: my life was lacking joy. I was so busy rushing from one commitment to the next, or knocking off items on my to-do lists, that I'd left no time to enjoy my days. And even during the times when it should have been easier to choose joy— while holidaying in beautiful places or spending time with loved ones—I was so anxious, so tied up in comparison, so focused on the future that I struggled to connect to the present moment enough to experience it in full colour. I couldn't be truly present because my understanding of happiness and joy was all wrong.

I believed that to be happy, to feel content with my life, I had to make all of the "right" decisions and meet society's expectations of me. I thought that if I just got a great job and travelled to the right places and made my life *appear* perfect, then something would click into place, and my feelings would catch up. I believed that happiness existed in a future version of my life and that I just had to tick off the right goals to get there. But with every promotion or milestone achieved, I didn't feel any happier—instead, I felt like I was moving further and further away from contentment and less confident that I'd ever get there.

My experience isn't unique. Maybe you're sitting there, reading this, feeling the same way. Maybe you, too, feel disconnected. Maybe you, too, are feeling rundown and exhausted. Maybe you, too, feel as though your life is lacking joy. So many of us fall into the trap of believing that happiness lies on the other side of a new job or a perfect partner or a much-desired vacation. And it's little wonder: we all grew up watching the same fairy tales—the ones I used to sell for a living, the ones that told us joy was reserved for the "happily ever after" and that we had to spend our lives striving to get there. Most of us didn't grow up in societies that taught us the importance of living a joyful life, and few of us had role models who showed us what that would look like. And so, it's easy to ignore the voices in our heads that say, "Surely life is supposed to feel better than this." It's easy to keep sucking it up. It's easy to keep sacrificing fulfilment and contentment for hustle and people pleasing and competition.

Many of us continue along this trajectory for decades, or even our entire lives, without making a change. I'd be on that path, too, if my world hadn't turned upside down in the summer of 2016. I'd poured so much time, energy, and effort into building this life that looked perfect on the outside, that I was reluctant to let it all come tumbling down, even if, in my clearest and most honest moments, I knew it wasn't making me happy. In fact, reluctant is probably a bit of an understatement; I was so keen to avoid change that I barely could admit to myself that I felt unfulfilled, much less build up the courage to voice that opinion to anybody else.

But in the summer of 2016, a huge, whirring, meteoric curveball crashed into my life, stripping me bare. Following a tragic accident, my beautiful cousin Blossom died when she was just four years old. In the span of a heartbeat, my life and the lives of the people I loved the most were irrevocably changed. So, too, were my beliefs about pretty much everything.

Since her death, I've read a lot about how grief or trauma can catalyse change, and that was certainly the case for me. Something I noticed almost instantly was how those cliché quotes we often scroll past on Instagram or Pinterest, the ones that say things like "Life is short" or "You only live once," took on new resonance. I was stripped of the naivety that accompanies youth, the innocence that gives us permission to keep delaying decisions or following the wrong path. I could no longer trick myself into thinking that everything would work itself out further down the line, because I had learned in the most brutal of ways that none of us know how much "line" we've got left. The experience taught me that life is finite, and that every second wasted is a second we can't get back. I was aware, perhaps for the first time ever, of just how alive I was, and I couldn't go on sleepwalking or shuffling from one miserable day to the next.

That time was the most difficult of my life, but ironically, it was also when I became obsessed with joy. Even as I battled my way through PTSD and deep grief, I was pulled by a sudden urgency to seize life. Amid a loss that felt truly senseless, making my life more joyful didn't so much feel like a choice but an obligation. Not seizing each day, not pursuing the things that would bring me joy, not making the most of the life I'd been given when so many other people don't get the chance, *that* felt disrespectful. Suddenly, those arbitrary metrics that I'd been so obsessed with—money, status, job titles—felt insignificant. Instead, I craved meaning and purpose and a deep sense of connection. Experiencing such a profound loss made me realise it wasn't enough to sit around and wait for some untold future date, or to cram all of my joy and happiness into a couple of weeks of vacation every year. I wanted to choose joy, to experience it every day, and so I set out to make that happen.

If you've picked up this book, chances are you, too, are ready to start choosing joy. Perhaps you're fed up with shuffling through your own life. Perhaps you're done trying to pretend that everything is perfect when it's actually making you sick and miserable. But the very thought of making changes, even joyful ones, might feel overwhelming. Maybe the collective grief and malaise of the last few years means you've lost touch with what joy feels like to you. Maybe you don't know where to start. You're not alone.

Of course, as I write about my own joy journey, it's easy to make it sound as if it was all a straightforward, linear process. It's tempting to rewrite history to make it seem as if I woke up one day, recovered from my grief, and changed my life, as easy as that. In reality, it was a slow, confusing, tricky process. A process that involved therapy and coaching and time spent engaging with other people's stories. A process that required me to start very small, to focus on teeny tiny slivers of joy and work my way up to the bigger changes. A process filled with self-doubt and impostor syndrome and countless tears. A process that often felt like taking one step forward and ten steps back.

But over time, that little seed, that tug to choose joy in some way every single day, changed my life. I started with small things, things that I didn't really believe could make much of a difference to my everyday life: writing gratitude lists, finding ten minutes each day to read a book, or going for a walk. But as momentum built, my confidence grew, and my experiments in choosing joy became increasingly bolder. I found new hobbies. I started to take better care of my health. I studied for a coaching qualification and started my own business. I quit my day job. I started volunteering. I redesigned my days in a way that kept joy as the North Star. I fell so hard for all things joyful and positive that I completed a master's in Applied Positive Psychology and Coaching Psychology and became The Joyful Coach. Nowadays, I get to spend my time helping people add more joy to their lives, whether that be through one-on-one coaching, delivering group programmes and workshops that help people to reconnect with their purposes and desires, or supporting companies in bringing joy back to the workplace.

Each new decision, each new choice to prioritise joy, felt scary and uncomfortable, but I couldn't stop because I was becoming happier. I was becoming kinder and more compassionate, both to myself and to others. I burnt out less frequently. I stopped dreading Monday mornings. I found it easier to appreciate everything that was good about my life, instead of dwelling on what I wanted to change. I ended my days feeling satisfied and joyful, instead of frustrated and exhausted. But best of all, I found a sense of peace—the type that can only come from knowing that I'm making the most of this precious time I've been given here on Earth.

I've learnt so much along the way that I'm desperate to share with you. We all deserve a life that feels truly joyful to us, and I'm passionate about helping people achieve a joyful life without first having to experience trauma or loss as a catalyst like I did. If you feel like that earlier version of me—lost, unsatisfied, tired, and full of guilt—you're in the right place. In the pages of this book, I'll help you to get started on your own joy journey, from understanding what a joyful life would look like for you, to making changes that will empower you to choose it every day. We'll explore what might have held you back so far, how to use tools to get to know yourself better, and how to start living in a more fun and inspired way. Guided by the latest research in positive psychology and behaviour change, we'll take the steps to transform you from burnt out to blooming. But first, let's explore two important questions . . .

What Exactly Is Joy?

As a trained positive psychology practitioner and researcher, I like to start any project by defining key terms and concepts. The slight trouble with this is that researchers and psychologists have yet to land on one unilateral definition of joy. Some describe it as a mood, while others describe it as an attitude, a change of perspective, or a trait, and there's no one set description of what joy feels like. What the research does agree on, though, is that contrary to popular belief, joy and happiness are not the same thing. In fact, it's clear that they are two separate constructs.

So, what are the differences? Let's start with happiness. Most will agree that happiness is a pleasant and desirable emotion, but it can often feel temporary or fleeting. As a Buddhist monk so beautifully put it, happiness can feel like a butterfly that lands on us and then flutters away. Whether or not we experience happiness is often circumstantial: we feel happy when we are on holiday or celebrating, or when we're surrounded by our loved ones, for example. In short, happiness tends to depend on external factors; it's an emotion that comes and goes based on the circumstances of life. Happiness happens to us.

Joy, on the other hand, is a choice. It is something that can always be cultivated, regardless of our circumstances. We can understand joy as more of a practice or an attitude than an emotion, and for that reason it can feel deeper than happiness. It can manifest as a sense of contentment or satisfaction, an experience of extreme delight, or deep peace. Joy can coexist with other emotions, too. Feeling sad or grief-stricken or anxious doesn't deny you access to joy.

You might have already experienced this—I certainly have. Perhaps you've been going through a hard time but still feel pure joy at something funny your kid says. Or perhaps you've been battling something tricky and still find contentment in the birds singing or the flowers colouring your garden. That's one of the reasons I get so excited about the work I do—we don't have to wait for life to change or improve to feel more joyful. We can start cultivating that feeling right now. We can start noticing and choosing joy today, regardless of what our lives look like.

Why Is Joy So Important?

Now that we have a characterisation of joy, let's delve into another question: Why is joy so important?

I get asked this question often, and I understand why. In a world filled with inequality, trauma, and gloomy news cycles, it can feel self-indulgent to focus on how joyful we feel. There are terrible injustices that require our attention, there are problems that need to be solved, there are glass ceilings that need to be shattered. We can fall into the trap of feeling helpless and hopeless, of thinking that there's no joy left to be had, or that we can put joy on the back burner until we've figured everything else out.

But, even amid the pain and drudgery, joy is still available to us, and the research tells us that joy and positivity are crucial ingredients for a satisfying and healthy life. Decades of study in the field of positive psychology have proven that prioritising positivity doesn't distract from the goals we have as individuals and as a society, but instead helps us to achieve them more quickly and effectively. Still not quite sold? Let me tell you more . . .

Let's begin with health, a topic that gets a lot of attention in our society and rightly so. Most of us can appreciate that joy has a positive impact on our mental health, but did you know that it can transform our physical health, too?

Studies have shown that joyful people have fewer chances of catching a cold and are less likely to have a heart attack. Research suggests that joy boosts our immune systems, and it can help to fight stress and pain (Nansook et al. 2016, 200-206). I certainly found this to be true—as joy began to grow in my own life, weeding out stress, the physical symptoms I'd been struggling with became more manageable, and some even completely disappeared. Perhaps most compelling is the research showing that joy can improve our chances of living a longer life. Let me repeat that again: being joyful improves our chances of living a longer life. Joy can actually give you more time. How incredible is that?

In addition to contributing to good health, joy is also proven to improve our relationships. Joy can help us to feel more socially connected by increasing our capacity for empathy and compassion. Plus, studies show that joy is contagious—sharing your joy with others can help them to experience it, too.

Next up, joy improves our chances of success. We might believe that achieving all of our career goals will make us happier, or that we'll have more time to prioritise joy once we've earned stacks of money, but research shows that the opposite is true: practising joy improves our cognitive functioning, resulting in a greater chance of being successful in our careers (Lyubomirsky, Sonja and King 2005, 803-855). Experiencing positive emotions can make us smarter, more resilient, and better at solving problems. Pretty cool, right?

Something that feels particularly important right now is the link between joy and resilience. Having a more joyful and positive mindset is thought to support adaptability and "bouncebackability," which can help you to recover from setbacks and curveballs more effectively. Joy has also been shown to be a protective factor for burnout. The more you prioritise joy, the less likely you are to suffer from exhaustion, depersonalisation, and apathy.

So, by prioritising our joy, by inviting more of it into our lives, we can be healthier, we can have happier relationships, we can be more successful, and we can build resilience. Joy is starting to sound pretty important, right? But for me, the most compelling reason for prioritising joy is this: we only get one short and precious life here on Earth. None of us are guaranteed anything more than what we have right here, right now. We aren't guaranteed better jobs or bigger houses. We aren't guaranteed perfect health. If we can't have control over all of our external circumstances, if we can't predict the future, aren't we better off focusing on finding our joy right now?

I'm excited to help you do just that.

About This Book

Many books will give you a formula for living a happier life. They'll provide you with lists of things to do, morning routines to follow, and changes to make. They'll give you a step-by-step plan, telling you that to live a more joyful life, all you need to do is follow it. This is not one of those books.

I believe that joy looks different for all of us. Just like success, there's no one right definition of joy—there's only the one that feels right for you. This book will help you turn inwards to discover your definition of joy, before helping you to figure out the changes you need to make to choose more of it every single day.

This book is split into three sections, and over the course of those sections, I'll guide you through the tried and tested framework that I use with my clients. In part one, "Start Where You Are," we'll take stock of where you are right now. We'll talk about some of the common mistakes we make when working towards positive changes, we'll evaluate what is and isn't bringing you joy right now, and we'll identify your values, which will serve as a personal road map as we move through the rest of the book. We'll also explore some of the key symptoms of burnout and overwhelm to understand how inviting more joy into our lives can combat these issues. This first section is all about deepening your understanding of who you are and where you are in your own joy journey right now. We can't make lasting, impactful change without that knowledge.

Here is the question I get asked most often as The Joyful Coach: How do I figure out what brings me joy? In part two of the book, "Finding Your Purpose and Joy," we'll clarify your definition of joy, explore how you can stay connected to it in a busy and noisy world, and understand the role of purpose in living a more joyful life. In this section, I'll guide you through powerful exercises to determine what would add more joy to your life, and how you can start to make changes that will invite more joy in.

Finally, in part three, "Creating Your Joyful Everyday," we'll put everything we've learned into action. In this section, we'll set goals that work for you, tackle some of the mindset blocks that hold us back, and make sure you have everything you need to stay the course. We'll look at the importance of experimenting, learn how to find joy during difficult periods, and bust the limiting beliefs that get in our way.

Throughout this book, you'll find recurring breakout sections designed to help you actualise everything you've learned. The "Try This" sections will give you tools to help you take action, while the "Attitude Hacks" are designed to help you change your perspective or try a new way of thinking. The "Reality Checks" will help you to ground what you're learning in real life, and the "Sprinkle of Joy" sections are designed to do just that—sprinkle some joy into your experience! Finally, each chapter ends with a "Let's Recap" section that summarises everything covered so far, and lined pages to write notes as you go along.

By the time you've finished this book, you'll have a greater understanding of yourself and what brings you joy, a personalised plan to help you create a more joyful life, and a whole host of tools and ideas to stay on track long after you've finished reading.

Here are some pointers to help you get the most from the book:

→ Be open and honest with yourself. It's tempting, when thinking about how we want our lives to be, to fall into the trap of "should." We get swept up in learned ideas of what we "should" be doing, desiring, or striving for. Instead, be open to seeing what shows up for you as you ponder joy. Use the lined writing pages throughout to complete the exercises and journaling prompts provided, and don't judge your dreams or hold yourself back. The only person you need to worry about pleasing is yourself.

→ Stay curious. As we'll explore throughout the book, so much of building a joyful life is noticing what does and doesn't bring you joy. Bring that attitude as you read, noticing what feels exciting to you, what feels challenging, what keeps showing up as you think about joy. Curiosity can be a great jumping-off point for positive change.

→ Have some fun! Building a joyful life is about *prioritising* more of the stuff that makes you feel good, and I hope that reading this book fits that bill. Enjoy the process—curl up somewhere cosy, make yourself something nice to drink, and savour this time that you're carving out for yourself.

Now let's get started . . .

ONE

START WHERE YOU ARE

CHAPTER 1

WHY DO I FEEL THIS WAY?

THE RISE OF BURNOUT

I knew that things had gotten bad when I was having cereal for dinner for the third night in a row. In my early twenties, on a tight budget and living for the weekend, I probably wouldn't have worried about such a diet, but as a married woman with a career and a mortgage, having cereal for dinner on a regular basis felt like a sign that something was seriously wrong.

It wasn't that I'd suddenly developed a deep love for Cheerios. It wasn't that I didn't know how to cook. The issue was that by the time I'd gotten up, made it through the workday, and commuted home, I didn't have a single drop of energy left to do anything other than pour cereal and milk into a bowl and eat it while standing at the counter. Then I'd spend the rest of the evening lying horizontally on the sofa, or in bed, watching mind-numbing television until I fell asleep.

It was autumn 2017, and as the nights drew on, my "get up and go" attitude began to drain away from me. I wasn't just tired or run down, suffering from the usual sluggishness that can accompany the colder months; I was completely devoid of energy and vitality. My to-do list grew longer every day, as even the simplest of tasks felt like mountains to climb. The fancy vitamins and expensive skincare products that I'd bought to make me look and feel a bit more alive sat in my bathroom cabinet untouched. The post piled up by the door unopened, WhatsApp messages from friends remained unanswered for weeks on end, and dust started to gather in every corner of the house. Every day, I got up and went to work, painting a face of normalcy, but even that was only because I was too worried about what might happen if I didn't.

When I look back now, I can see with glittering clarity that I was struggling with burnout, but at the time, I had no idea why I was feeling the way I was. I was constantly searching for the cause of my malaise. I told myself it was the post-wedding comedown, something that friends had warned me would happen after I'd gotten married that summer. I told myself that it was a hangover from my experience of grief, even though I'd been feeling much better earlier in the year, after regular counselling and therapy. I even tried to convince myself that the way I was feeling was nothing special, that it was just part of being an adult in the working world, and that everyone around me was feeling the same way. I assumed that this was just how life was supposed to be, and that's why no one seemed to be talking about it.

Perhaps my description of how I felt back then resonates with you. Maybe you're feeling exhausted, both mentally and physically, from the last few years and all of the uncertainty and change that came with them. Maybe you're feeling overwhelmed, pulled in many directions, struggling to meet the constant demands on your time. Perhaps you're finding it difficult to connect with the things that once added joy and meaning to your life. Or maybe you can't even remember what those things were. Perhaps your inner critic is louder than ever, pointing out all of the mistakes you've made and all the ways in which you're falling behind. Maybe you're feeling cynical.

If any of those statements speak to you, you're likely experiencing some sort of burnout. Burnout has become a bit of a buzzword in the last few years because more of us are suffering from it than ever before. According to the World Health Organization (WHO), burnout is characterised by three distinct symptoms:

→ *Feelings of energy depletion and exhaustion:* always feeling tired, no matter how much sleep or rest you get

→ *Feelings of negativity or cynicism:* struggling to find the silver linings, experiencing a sense that no matter what you do, nothing will make a difference

→ *Reduced performance:* struggling to achieve at the same standards you previously met

The cause of burnout is clear: excessive and prolonged periods of unmanaged stress. When we break down the meaning of stress, it's clear why we've all been more susceptible to it in recent years. Stress is defined as a psychological, physiological, and behavioural reaction that occurs when individuals perceive that they cannot adequately handle the demands upon them. When the to-do lists feel overwhelming, when we're faced with uncertainty, or when we're asked to do things that we don't feel equipped for, our bodies, brains, and behaviours are impacted in some way. Depending on how we view the demands placed upon us, nearly everything has the potential to cause stress, from last-minute requests from your boss and arguments with your partner, to grappling with climate change and navigating societal expectations.

Make a list of the things that feel stressful in your life. What is it that feels so stressful about those things? What is the main cause of the stress? Here are a couple of examples:

Example 1:

❊ **Stressor:** A current work project.

❊ **What is it that feels stressful?** Hitting the deadline for the project when I already have a full workload.

❊ **What is the main cause of stress?** The unrealistic deadline set by my boss.

Example 2:

❊ **Stressor:** Planning a wedding.

❊ **What is it that feels stressful?** Managing different suppliers and trying to make the day as enjoyable as possible for guests.

❊ **What is the main cause of stress?** My expectation that the day needs to be perfect.

Now, take a moment to reflect on how burnout shows up in your life. While many of us experience burnout, how that burnout presents differs for each of us. Journal about burnout using the following prompts:

❊ What is your experience of burnout?

❊ Can you identify the stressors that led to your burnout?

❊ What are your telltale signs and signals that you're approaching burnout?

❊ What has helped you to manage or recover from burnout in the past?

Stress isn't always a bad thing. In fact, a little bit of stress (what psychologists call eustress) can be good for us and our performance, because eustress releases chemicals and hormones that make us more alert and energetic. If you're interviewing for a job, running a race, or sitting an exam, you probably want to experience a little bit of stress, as it will sharpen your focus, inspire more creativity, and enable you to reach peak performance. Similarly, our stress responses are vital during times of emergency—it's the experience of stress that propels us to take survival-enhancing action.

But trouble arises when stress becomes chronic, intense, and frequent with little time for your body and mind to recover. Unfortunately, that's where a lot of us find ourselves. A UK-based study led by YouGov in 2018 found that a whopping seventy-four percent of people reported feeling so stressed in the past year that they had been overwhelmed or unable to cope (Mental Health Foundation 2018). Mind you, this study took place before the pandemic and the extra worries and pressures that came along. Unmanaged, these chronic periods of stress can lead to burnout.

Burnout shows up differently for all of us, but we each have telltale signs. Ignoring those signs and continuing to push through can lead to catastrophic consequences. Burnout isn't something that will simply go away on its own, so the longer we ignore it, the more likely it is to build and manifest in other ways, from physical illness to serious mental health issues.

There are lots of books out there that will give you a step-by-step guide to managing your burnout. They'll tell you to set better boundaries and switch off notifications on your phone, to scale back your work commitments and only answer your emails during certain hours. That is all good advice, but I wanted to offer up a slightly different solution, one with more staying power: prioritising joy.

What Does Joy Have To Do With Burnout?

What does joy have to do with burnout? I'm so glad you asked. One of the reasons I'm so passionate about helping people learn to live a more joyful life is that research reveals joy to be a protective factor against burnout. The more we prioritise and experience joy in our lives, the less likely we are to experience burnout and the negative side effects that accompany it.

The most obvious reason for this is that joy provides some relief from the stress we experience in our day-to-day lives. When we do something that creates a sense of joy and contentment—whether it be hanging out with loved ones, spending time in nature, or engaging with art and culture—we give our brains and bodies a break from the cortisol released when we feel stressed or under pressure. This gives us the opportunity to recover from the physiological and psychological impacts of stress, reducing the risk of burning out.

But there is even greater value in experiencing positive emotions such as joy, particularly when it comes to building resilience and adaptability in the face of stress. According to prominent social psychologist Barbara Fredrickson, while negative emotions can prompt us to employ narrow, survival-oriented behaviours (such as engaging the fight, flight, or freeze responses), positive thoughts and emotions broaden our awareness and encourage new thoughts and actions. Her broaden-and-build theory explains that when we experience positive emotions such as joy, we broaden our thinking, allowing us to draw on a wide range of possible solutions and behaviours, therefore building a whole host of mental resources, including resilience, that help us to live enhanced, healthier, and more fulfilling lives (Fredrickson 2004). The more we experience those positive emotions, the greater the benefits.

When I was at my most burnt out, joy felt more distant than it had ever been before. I didn't understand the science behind positive emotions back then, but I knew intuitively that something needed to change. My burnout was making me miserable, and worse, I felt that life was passing me by without me really *living* it. I adopted a new mantra: lean into what feels good. That mantra became an intention that I turned to hundreds of times a day. There were no big overnight switches, no grand gestures, just a gentle leaning into the things that felt good—breathing a bit of fresh air, reading a chapter of a book, listening to some of my favourite songs while I cooked dinner. In time, leaning into those things, finding those tiny slivers of joy, helped me to re-connect to myself and the things I loved, to regain the optimism and energy that had once been my norm.

The stress I was experiencing didn't go away, but making time for the things that brought me joy helped me to build my resilience. I could better cope with the pressures of life. And I benefited from that positive upwards spiral, too. While at first those positive emotions and slivers of joy were relatively small or hard to come by, the more I made space for them, the easier to access they became, and so the benefits of those positive emotions felt heightened, too. In time, I was able to strive for more joy, ultimately leading me to the place where I made some big, life-changing shifts, such as retraining and pivoting into a brand-new career.

ATTITUDE HACK

Often when life gets stressful, the things that help us feel our best fall to the bottom of the to-do list. We skip the yoga class to meet the work deadline, and we miss out on sleep to juggle our busy social lives. We put joy on the back burner while we take care of everyone else.

This can feel like a logical response. After all, there's only so much time in the day, and sometimes we have to let things slide. But evidence suggests that we can increase our capacity to deal with the demands of life—and avoid burnout in the process—when we balance our demands with the resources we have to cope with those demands.

Imagine getting ready to take a road trip. You wouldn't set off on your journey without first filling your car with fuel, and the more fuel you put in the car, the farther you'll be able to go. The same is true of our lives—the more we pursue activities that energise us, the more fuel we have available for the tasks and activities that drain us. If we go too long without topping up the energy tank, we end up burning out. As life gets more demanding, we need more, not less, of the stuff that makes us feel good.

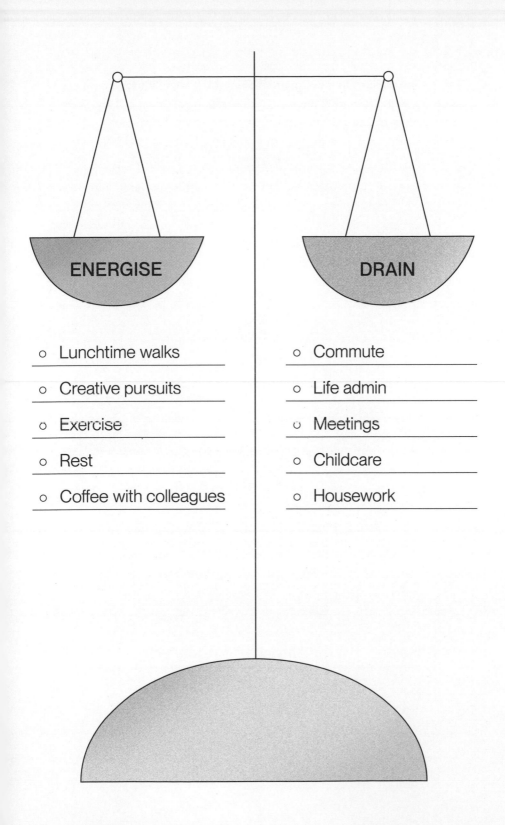

ENERGISE

- Lunchtime walks
- Creative pursuits
- Exercise
- Rest
- Coffee with colleagues

DRAIN

- Commute
- Life admin
- Meetings
- Childcare
- Housework

Take a few minutes to make a list of all of the things that top your energy up. Include as many activities and tasks as you can think of, from your basic needs (e.g., sleep, movement, food, fresh air) to your interests or hobbies (like scrapbooking, horseback riding, hiking, or baking). There are no right or wrong answers, only the things that make *you* feel good.

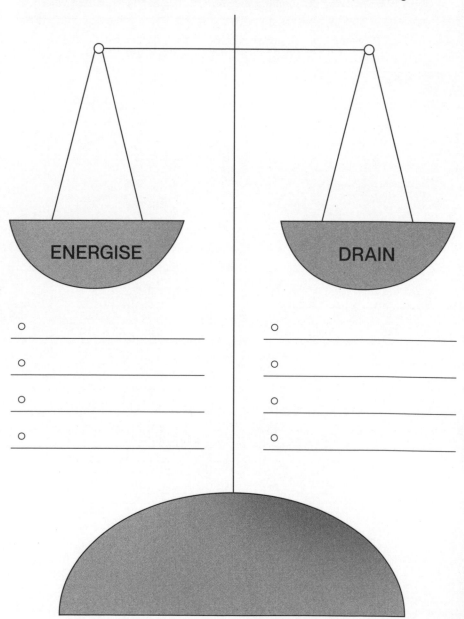

It's Not Your Fault You Feel Like This

If you're feeling burnt out right now, if you feel tired or overwhelmed or stuck in a rut, know this: it isn't your fault. Experiencing burnout isn't a sign of weakness. It's a natural response to dealing with high, unrelenting levels of stress. We are living through unprecedented times and that comes with a hefty bucket of stress, and that's before you look at the other factors that can make life feel even more challenging. If you belong to a marginalised community, work in highly stressful conditions, or face poverty, for example, you will likely bear a heavier load.

But it's not that joy is some sort of magic wand, that inviting more of it into our lives will fix everything. Prioritising our own joy will not make microaggressions disappear, reduce barriers to success, or disintegrate the injustices woven into our systems. The goal of this book isn't to add to the growing narrative of toxic positivity, perpetuating the idea that if our lives are difficult, it's just because we're not being positive enough. That approach doesn't help anyone, and it doesn't lead to the structural change so desperately needed.

No, more joy won't fix everything. But it will empower you. It will fortify you and make you stronger. It will give you an outlet for things that make you feel most alive. Joy will remind you of your worth, it will connect you to what is most important in your life, and it will empower you to build resilience, so that you are better equipped to deal with the stress and chaos of twenty-first-century life.

Joy alone won't dismantle our burnout culture, but there's no denying that it's an incredibly useful tool, and better still, it's one that puts power and autonomy back in our hands. It's no selfish thing, either—change requires optimism, and in prioritising our joy, we can find the energy, creativity, and determination required to fight for greater justice and tackle the wider systemic changes that need to happen. Bring it on.

LET'S RECAP

✳ More of us are suffering from burnout than ever before.

✳ Burnout occurs as a result of excessive and prolonged periods of unmanaged stress.

✳ Prioritising joy can help us to better manage stress and improve our resilience, helping to protect us from burnout.

✳ Balancing our demands with the resources we have to cope with them can help us manage our energy.

falling at the first hurdle

CHAPTER 2

WHERE WE GO WRONG WHEN TRYING TO CHANGE

Now that we've talked about the power of joy in tackling burnout and over-whelm, you might be itching to start making positive, joyful changes. Before we do that, I want to start by asking you a question . . .

Hands up if you've ever promised yourself that you're going to make a change for the better, and then failed?

I'll guess that more than a few of you are sitting there with your hands raised. I'll admit that I've got both of mine thrust firmly in the air. And we're not alone—studies show that many of us fail to achieve the goals we set for ourselves, with some research estimating that over eighty percent of us struggle to keep our resolutions.

Though I've dedicated my career to supporting others to live their most joyful lives, choosing joy in my own life hasn't always come naturally to me. You might assume that for a coach, making positive changes is something that feels easy and pain-free. But I have failed many, many times at making a change. For years I was stuck in a near-constant cycle of boom and bust, setting goals or intentions and pursuing them with gusto, before inevitably burning out and giving up. Every Monday I'd start afresh with a new health kick or habit change, and every Friday I'd end up right back where I started, only feeling even more miserable and cynical.

I dug through some of my old journals and diaries to share with you some of my own personal goal failures. Though this list isn't exhaustive, I hope it reminds you that every path is marked with failures, even those (or maybe especially) of experts.

→　I failed to keep attending the gym that I paid a small fortune to join.

→　I failed to learn more than a handful of Spanish words, despite downloading Duolingo and setting many calendar reminders to practise verb conjugations.

→　I failed to get past the first chapter of so many of the "must-read" classic books.

→ I failed to figure out how to use my digital camera properly, despite paying a sizable sum for an online course in digital photography.

→ I failed to stick to any one of the many, many diets I started every Monday morning. I must have tried at least twenty.

→ I failed at getting multiple businesses off the ground, including a jewellery business and a local career networking platform.

→ I failed to write a novel. Honestly, I failed to write even a single scene.

Sifting through these goals and intentions in those old journals stirred up so many memories and emotions. I can vividly remember how I approached each of these projects and goals filled with energy and motivation. How optimistic I felt as I wrote them down in my diary or thought about the changes I wanted to make. I can remember how confident I felt as I bought the kit, decided on my plan of action, and threw myself into becoming the type of person I thought I was going to be. I can remember how certain I was every Monday morning that *this* was the time it was going to be different, that *this* was the time I'd finally manage to make it stick.

And yet, time and time again, I'd fail. Sometimes I'd barely get out of the blocks, and other times I'd manage to last a week, two weeks, maybe even three, before eventually giving up. But I kept on failing, and with each new failure, I'd experience a fresh sting of shame. Shame that had me shrinking away when loved ones asked how I was getting on. Shame that washed over me every time I saw an unread book on the shelf or opened a cupboard to find the ingredients for some low carb meal I knew I was never going to eat. Shame that, over time, chipped away at my resilience and self-worth. With each new failure, a narrative started to form: I didn't deserve to feel happy if I couldn't even muster the willpower to push through with the goals I'd set for myself.

I knew that this cycle of boom and bust was unhealthy, and I knew it wasn't helping me to make lasting progress, as I always ended up back at square one. But I couldn't see where I was going wrong. I was setting clear goals, goals that were *smart* and objective. I was committing to those goals, sharing my intentions with my loved ones, and asking them to provide me with some gentle accountability. I was listening to podcasts and reading books about motivation and ambition, I was scheduling the time in my diary to work on my actions, and I had the support of my husband and friends who were always cheering me on. More and more, I started to feel as though I was the issue. Sound familiar?

Our Brains Don't Always Know What's Best For Us

What I know now, after years of studying behaviour change and positive psychology, is that I had no chance of finding the motivation to achieve those goals I was setting, because they weren't things I truly wanted in the first place. I'd tried my best to convince myself that I did, and sometimes it worked. But those goals were always influenced by some external force. They were goals I'd set for myself in trying to keep up with my peers. They were goals I was striving for to make my life appear shinier on the outside. They were goals that came from a place of comparison and fear, instead of from a genuine desire to make my life more fulfilling and joyful.

I wanted to learn Spanish because I thought it would make me look smarter if I could speak another language. I wanted to be a bit thinner because I thought it would make it seem like I had my life together. I wanted to be good at photography or have a successful jewellery business because I thought it would make me seem creative and cool. Not once did I stop to consider whether I truly *wanted* any of these things. I knew that I was unhappy. I knew that I needed to make a change. But I never stopped to consider what that change should be. When it came to inviting more joy into my life, I'd tripped on the first hurdle.

So many of us do. We start new years or new months or new weeks armed with long lists of fresh goals, resolutions, and the best of intentions. We feel determined that *this time* will be the time we commit to change, that *this goal* will be the goal that finally makes life feel a bit more fulfilling. But when we place all our hopes on our latest resolutions, only to struggle to make them stick, we feel crushed. We internalise the failure and see ourselves as the issue. Our confidence, self-esteem, and sense of worthiness take a hit. We become our own biggest critics—nothing saps our joy quicker than walking around with a mean voice inside our heads, chattering away all day.

I see this a lot with my coaching clients. They'll often spend our first call together telling me about all of the times they've tried to make a change in the past, and all the reasons they've failed. They'll tell me that they're lazy, that they struggle with motivation, that they're not as smart or creative or committed as their friends or peers. They'll tell me that they just don't have the willpower required to achieve their hopes and dreams. And I sit there, listening quietly, knowing that never once in my years of coaching have I found these damning self-indictments to be true. The very act of striving for a more joyful life and having the willingness to get there shows that we possess motivation, creativity, and determination in buckets. So, if that's not the problem, what is? What's really getting in the way of us making a positive change that lasts? Usually, it's that we're setting goals that don't truly inspire us, thus encountering resistance along the way.

You might be feeling a little bit confused. Why would we set ourselves goals that we didn't want to achieve? Why would we be drawn towards things that wouldn't improve our lives? Why would we bother striving for stuff that wouldn't make us feel more satisfied? Well, in my experience, this is usually where comparison or our desire to "keep up" comes in. Although social media is often blamed for the harmful effects of social comparison, our desire for connection and validation has existed just as long as humans have. We're wired to compare ourselves to others for survival—it was one of the ways that our earliest ancestors kept themselves safe. To survive, we needed to belong to a pack, and therefore, we were constantly looking at the people around us and sizing ourselves up to them to make sure we were fitting in. This need to belong was so imperative to our survival that it became hard-wired into our brains, and it hasn't gone away. Instead, it's become easier than ever to compare ourselves, not only to the people in our immediate communities, but to just about anyone in the world.

Our brains use this information to form a picture of what is most desirable or acceptable in the worlds in which we exist. All the data we gather about what's good or right or cool influences and shapes our ambitions and goals. As a result, we get swept up in who we think we *should be*, rather than giving ourselves permission to fully embrace who we are. Our goals and beliefs about ourselves are informed by society's expectations or other people's opinions, and as a result, we end up striving for stuff that doesn't truly inspire us. And the scary thing is that this process happens almost completely subconsciously, meaning that we're often not aware of the influence the outside world has on our inner narrative. It happens on autopilot: we see someone smiling on a sunny beach and internalise the idea that we'd be happier if we booked that vacation. We see someone celebrating their latest job promotion on LinkedIn, and we start to entertain the idea that the thing missing from our lives is career progression.

I can see so clearly how this process played out in my own life when I think back on some of those goals I'd set for myself. For example, I felt like I *should* set a goal of losing weight, not because I wanted to improve my health or my connection with my body, but because I'd grown up in a society that showed me that thin people were more likable or successful. I thought I *should* be building a jewellery business or writing a novel, not because I had an innate talent or calling to work on those projects, but because I'd internalised the idea that creative jobs were so much cooler than the ones I was interested in. Instead of taking the time to think about what would truly make me feel more fulfilled or add more joy to my life, I let those "shoulds" lead the way. I fooled myself into thinking that happiness would come once I finally morphed myself into someone else, instead of embracing the person I already was. I tricked myself into believing that the things that made other people happy would satisfy me too, instead of recognising that we are all unique, complex beings with our own wants and desires.

ATTITUDE HACK

Consider a time when you set a goal for yourself and failed to achieve it. What motivated you to set that goal? How did you hope life would change if you achieved it?

Now, try to look at that failure with kinder, more compassionate eyes. Why might you have struggled to achieve that goal? Why might that particular goal not have been right for you in that season of life?

Try not to dwell too much on those past failures. Instead, learn from them, then let them go.

Where You Get Your Motivation From Matters

When we fall into the trap of believing that we can achieve our way to happiness or find joy by impressing other people, we set ourselves up to fall at the first hurdle. Researchers have shown that to change our behaviours, extrinsic motivation (the desire to complete a task to receive a reward or meet others' expectations) is not enough (Ryan 2000, 54-67). Instead, reaching goals requires intrinsic motivation: we need to find satisfaction and fulfilment in the process of working on our goals, not just as a result of accomplishing them. When we rely on extrinsic motivation to help us make a change, not only do we spend precious energy and life minutes pursuing someone else's standards for joy, but we diminish the chances of achieving our goals. We set ourselves up to fail, and then when we do inevitably fail, it hurts. It hurts our pride, it knocks our confidence, and it jades our worldview, making us increasingly miserable and sceptical. And that scepticism is dangerous, because over time, it makes us believe that change isn't an option, that pursuing more joy is futile, that this is as good as it gets. Instead, we need to develop a sense of intrinsic motivation, identifying the changes or activities that will feel internally rewarding to pursue. When we do that, we end up with goals that not only feel more authentic and exciting to us, but also that we're more motivated to achieve, even when things get tough.

Realising that I was missing this intrinsic motivation was a pivotal moment for me. Rather than a lightbulb moment, I noticed a gradual awareness that the approach I'd taken wasn't working for me. Gently, old beliefs began to unravel as I started to question what I'd been taught about what makes a "good life." Despite the setbacks and confidence knocks I'd suffered, there was still a tiny seed of optimism, a sliver of hope that life could be better. I'd tried to do life the traditional way—I'd tried striving for all of the things I thought would make me happier—and I'd failed. But I hadn't completely lost hope. I was willing to try one more thing: getting intentional.

Intention is how we break the cycle. It's the magic ingredient that empowers us to step away from the constant boom and bust, to cease the never-ending dance between beginning and giving up. Intention allows us to inject some authenticity into the goal-setting process. When we invite intention to the party, we acknowledge the fact that we are all unique, complex individuals, with our own desires and ambitions. We honour that there is no one-size-fits-all approach to life. There's no universal blueprint for joy—only the one that feels right to us, that respects who we are and who we truly want to be.

So, how do we do that? How do we reconnect with who we are, and start to be more intentional in our approach to goal setting? We start by taking stock, by checking in, by getting a handle on what is and isn't working before we launch into making a change. We start by considering how we want our life *to feel*, rather than just making a list of the things we want.

> ✦ A Sprinkle OF JOY ✦
>
> Give yourself permission to do something simply because you enjoy the process of it. In our fast-paced, hyper-productive world, we rarely slow down to do something purely for the fun of it. Challenge yourself to do exactly that today.

A Tool To Help You

If we haven't spent a lot of time connecting with our intuition and being intentional about how we want to live, it can be difficult to know where to start. A tool that can help is something I like to call the joy wheel. It's a simple tool, but it can be effective at helping us to look at our lives as a whole, taking a snapshot of what is and isn't feeling good right now. This is incredibly valuable information to have when it comes to considering what will make our lives feel more joyful. It can also help us to measure over time whether the changes we're making are having the desired impact.

First, give each of the wheel's eight spokes a label that corresponds with the eight most important areas of your life—things like health, family, work, and career development. Then, give each area of your life a score from zero to ten for how satisfied you feel in that area, with ten being completely satisfied, and zero being completely unsatisfied. Mark those scores on each spoke. Finally, draw a line between each mark, and you'll be left with a clear picture of what is and isn't feeling good for you right now. We can then use this knowledge in the next section as we start to identify the changes that will make our lives more joyful.

(example)
Joy Wheel

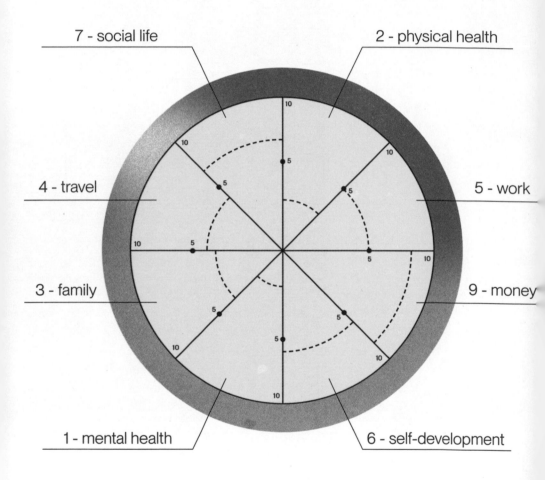

Your Joy Wheel

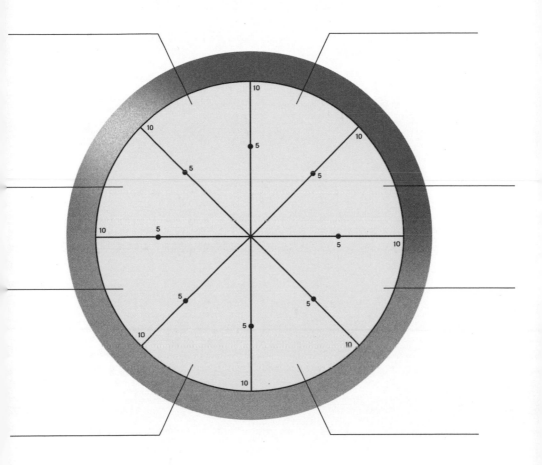

If you'd like to explore the idea of the joy wheel further, the following prompts can be a great jumping-off point for some further digging. There's no right or wrong way to use these prompts—you could answer the questions in your journal, use them as conversation starters with a friend, or simply mull them over as you go about your day. The idea is simply to continue this process of connecting to who you are and how you want your life to be, so that you can bring some intention to your joy journey.

How does your life feel right now? Try to describe it with three to five words.

How would you prefer your life to feel? Again, try to identify three to five words.

What areas of your life feel joyful?

What areas of your life feel more challenging?

Make a list of times you've experienced joy in the last few months. Do the things on your list have anything in common?

When do you feel most content?

If there's one thing I want you to take away from this chapter, it's a little bit of compassion for yourself and those previous failures at making a change. Those failures don't define you (just as my failure to speak Spanish or to regularly attend the gym doesn't define me). They simply reaffirm that you're a human living in a messy, complicated, noisy world.

It's important that we try to let go of these failures, that we practise some gratitude for the lessons they've taught us, and set them free, so that we can create some space for the joyful changes on the horizon. Joy requires levity that's hard to access when we're weighed down by regret and self-criticism.

LET'S RECAP

✳   When it comes to making a change, intrinsic motivation is more powerful than extrinsic motivation.

✳   We often set ourselves up to fail when we set goals related to the people we think we "should" be, instead of the people we truly are.

✳   To make impactful changes that last, we need to focus on setting goals that feel more authentic and that resonate internally, instead of looking outside of ourselves for inspiration.

✳   Getting to know ourselves better and using the information we already have about our lives will inform our next steps.

What really matters

CHAPTER 3

most

IDENTIFYING YOUR CORE VALUES

In the last chapter, we explored the importance of measuring how your life currently feels before identifying the joyful changes you want to make. There's one more tool I want to share with you to help you do just that.

Enter: values. When I work with my one-on-one coaching clients, we start with identifying their values and how closely aligned with those values their life feels. My clients often tell me that it's this work that they refer back to most often when we've finished working together.

Knowing what your values are can be incredibly powerful when building a joyful life. In this chapter, we'll explore why, before getting to grips with what yours are.

What Are Values?

Our values are the levers that drive the decisions we make and the actions we take. Whether we know it or not, we all have a set of core values that shape who we are and what we do. And they are unique to each of us; we can think of them as a sort of blueprint for our authentic selves.

Knowing our values can provide us with incredibly useful information when building a joyful life, because the more aligned our life is to our values, the happier we'll be. But few of us are aware that we have these core values, and even fewer could articulate with confidence what they are. If we don't know our own values, we make decisions without consulting them, which often leads to a life that looks great on the outside but feels unsatisfying and unfulfilling on the inside.

That's what happened to me. When I graduated from uni, I worked my backside off to get what I thought was going to be my dream job, and yet, despite the movie premieres and the free tickets to Disneyland, I was miserable. And I felt so guilty about that. I was one of the lucky ones—I had a good salary, a generous benefits package, and a lovely team who genuinely cared about my development. What did I have to complain about? But despite my self-flagellation, those negative feelings didn't go away. I'd spend all week counting down the days until Friday, and then before I knew it, the Sunday blues would come rolling in. I couldn't shake the feeling that I didn't fit, that something was missing. I tried everything to fill that hole, to try to quell the unease of feeling in the wrong place. I shadowed other teams to see if I'd fit better in a different department. I took on extra projects to add some variety to my days. I tried focusing on the parts of the job I enjoyed the most, but nothing worked. I still felt like I didn't quite belong.

It was only a few years later, when I started working with a coach to uncover my core values, that I was able to see what the issue was. While my jobs in the corporate world ticked all of the boxes of traditional success, and while they garnered lots of positive feedback and respect from my loved ones and peers, they weren't remotely aligned with my own values. One of my core values is freedom, which massively conflicted with the reality of being stuck in an office from nine a.m. to six p.m. every day. And my values of creativity and connection were seriously underutilised as I spent my days with my head stuck in spreadsheets or performing repetitive tasks. Finally, understanding that my job didn't align with my values helped release those feelings of guilt. There was nothing wrong with the job or company I'd ended up in, and there was nothing wrong with me; but our values didn't fit.

What Do Values Have To Do With Joy?

Identifying and understanding our values is a crucial part of building a joyful life. When we aren't living our lives in alignment with our core values, we experience some sort of conflict. That conflict can start to cause issues. It can lead us to compare and despair, reduce our motivation and zest for life, and lead to poor mental and physical health. As we learned in Chapter One, when we experience those negative emotions and symptoms, it's not only difficult to experience joy, but to envisage how we can make positive changes.

Our values also provide us with our own personal road maps for joy. The more closely aligned we are to our core values, the more joyful, content, and satisfied we'll feel, and the easier it will be to make decisions that feel authentic and congruent to us. In a noisy world filled with expectations and other people's opinions of what should make us happy, determining and using our values can help us to stay connected to who we are and what fulfils us.

Finding Your Values

There are a few ways to determine your values. I'll share with you the process that I walk all of my one-on-one clients through.

Step 1

I start by inviting my clients to journal on the following prompts.

1. **Think about the last time you experienced a flow state. What were you doing? Who were you with? What was your environment like?**

    You can think of flow states as being "in the zone." "Flow" refers to the feeling of complete immersion in whatever task or activity you're engaged in. Usually, flow states occur when you're experiencing enjoyment but also feeling a little bit challenged.

2. **Recall your five happiest moments from the last year. Why did they bring you so much joy? What common themes run through those moments?**

    To answer this question most effectively, consider when you were happiest in the last year. Sometimes we can be drawn to list the moments when we might have looked the happiest, or when we might have expected ourselves to be happy, instead of really considering when we've experienced the most joy. Try to avoid those moments of expected happiness in favour of listing the moments you truly felt happy.

3. **If you had to prioritise just three things in your life, what would they be?**

    We all have more than three things that are important in our lives, but this question is designed to help you think about what is truly most important to you.

4. **Consider what you want to be known for. How do you want to make other people feel? What do you want to be said about you when you're not in the room?**

    The question has less to do with how we experience life and more to do with what we want our reputation to be. This can be a powerful way of connecting with what we value and the impact we want to have.

5. **Make a list of your five proudest achievements. What is it about those achievements that resonates most with you?**

Just as with question two, challenge yourself to think about what you're truly most proud of, instead of what other people are proud of you for. It can be helpful to consider some of the less measurable achievements, too. For example, you might feel proud of the relationships you have with your family or the way you coped during a difficult time.

Step 2

Once you've had time to think about and answer these questions, give yourself some space. You might want to head out for a little walk or even close your notebook for the day and come back to it later in the week. The aim is to create a distance between you and what you've written, so that you can return to read your answers with fresh eyes.

When you're ready, the next step is to look for themes within your answers and use these to identify your values. Are there certain words or phrases that keep cropping up? Are there connections between your answers that feel important? What feels most present in what you've written?

The aim is to analyse your answers and use them to help you identify five to seven core values that sum up who you are and what is important to you. It will be tempting to write a longer list, and of course there will be more than five to seven things that are important to you, but for our values to help us to make decisions and impact change, we need a honed list.

To get you started, I've included a list of values to the right. This list is by no means exhaustive, and you should choose words not included here if they resonate with you, but this should provide a bit of inspiration to get you started. Once you've reviewed this list of examples, use the chart on page 49 to write down your own.

EXAMPLE VALUES

accountability	happiness
achievement	health
ambition	independence
assertiveness	inner harmony
authenticity	integrity
balance	intelligence
belonging	intuition
challenge	joy
community	love of learning
compassion	love
contribution	loyalty
creativity	play
curiosity	practicality
decisiveness	prosperity
determination	resourcefulness
discipline	security
diversity	selflessness
empathy	sensitivity
endurance	serenity
enthusiasm	spirituality
equality	spontaneity
excitement	stability
exploration	strength
family	success
freedom	thoughtfulness
fun	variety
generosity	wisdom

Some Pointers to Help You

→ It can be tempting to choose the values that feel most aspirational or exciting. Instead, try to pick the ones that feel most true to you. If you end up with a list of values that aren't an authentic fit, the changes or shifts you make in accordance with them may result in more conflict rather than more joy.

→ It's okay if your values don't feel neat and complementary, so long as they feel authentic to you. For example, two of my values are freedom and security. If we buy into the traditional meanings of these words, those values might feel at odds with each other. But I know that to feel my most joyful self, I need both the freedom to live and work in a way that feels good to me, and the security to know I can pay my bills each month. Your interpretation of your values is important, so don't dismiss them just because they don't fit into a neat box.

→ If you're struggling to whittle your values down, imagine which would cause the most discomfort in your life if you weren't able to align with it. There might be some things you care about but can live without, whereas other things will feel vital for you to flourish.

→ Try to let go of what other people have told you about yourself. There's no qualification of values other than knowing that they're important and motivating to you. For example, a core value of mine is creativity. I don't have a traditional creative job, and I'm not very good at arts or crafts, but I know that when my ability to think or act creatively is stifled, I experience conflict and challenge.

→ You'll know that you've arrived at your list of core values when reading them feels like reading an introduction to who you are and what's most important to you. You should be able to recognise yourself in those words.

YOUR LIST OF VALUES

1. _____

2. _____

3. _____

4. _____

5. _____

6. _____

7. _____

Using Your Values To Help You Find More Joy

Now that we've identified your core values, it's time to explore how to use them to invite more joy into your life. We're going to do this in two ways: checking in with how aligned they are with your current reality, and then exploring how we can use our values to make more joyful decisions.

Let's start by checking in. The idea here is to measure our lives as they are now against the values we've identified. Just as with the joy wheel in the last chapter, this exercise can give us a quick snapshot of what is and isn't working in our lives right now. It will help us to identify areas of focus when it comes to thinking about the changes that will invite more joy into our lives.

To start, review your list of values, and then give each value a score out of ten for how aligned you currently feel to it, with ten being perfectly aligned, and zero being not at all. Try not to overthink this one—whatever number comes to mind first is probably the right one.

Then, take some time to reflect on the following questions:

→ Which of your values do you feel most aligned with at the moment?

→ Which of your values do you feel least aligned with at the moment?

→ What would have to change in your life to score ten out of ten for each value?

→ If you were to score ten out of ten for each value, how would you feel?

→ What is currently holding you back from putting your values into action more?

Try not to worry too much if your scores are low or your current reality feels far removed from your core values. Many people find themselves in that boat—myself included when I first completed this exercise! It just means there's plenty we can do to add more joy to your life, and that's exactly what we'll be exploring in future chapters.

(✸ *Try* This ✸)

If this is the first time you've done any introspective work like this, it can feel challenging and intimidating. This exercise might feel tricky if you've never really given much thought to what drives you or what is most important to you. But that's okay—it's difficult because it's new, not because you're doing it wrong. Try to let go of any perfectionist tendencies, and instead lean into the process and see this as an opportunity to get to know yourself a little better. For each of your core values, make a list of things you could start doing right now to bump the score up by one or two points. We're not talking huge shifts here, just a few little things you could start to do right away to invite more joy into your life. Try to commit to at least one or two actions.

For example, if connection is one of your core values, you could schedule a long phone call with your best friend or strike up a conversation with your barista. If creativity is important to you, you could carve out an hour or two to work on a craft project or explore a more creative way to solve a problem at work.

Starting to put your values into action will keep them present in your mind, empowering you to feel more aligned and grounded in your day-to-day life.

Decision-Making

Finally, let's examine how to use our values to make better, more joyful decisions. To illustrate this, I'll share a story from my own life.

Three years ago, I was sitting at my desk when a notification pinged on my screen: my boss had scheduled an impromptu one-on-one meeting for later that morning. At the time, I was working at a tech start-up, where I'd worked for two years. It was a fun job in the beauty sector, which gave me access to lots of free skincare goodies. The company had an energetic culture, and I was leading a team of over eighty brilliant people. And yet, I still felt that same lack of belonging that I'd experienced in roles at other companies.

It had been a couple of years since my big burnout, and I'd gotten much better at prioritising joy and setting more authentic goals, but I knew I still had a way to go. More recently, I'd been exploring the idea of changing careers—working with coaches and mentors and starting to complete a new qualification in my evenings and weekends. I'd even started my own podcast sharing my experience and discussing all things positivity and joy. I'd committed to trying something new, but I was still very much a beginner. My day job took up most of my time and energy, and everything else was relegated to the side hustle territory.

I didn't know what to expect when I walked into that meeting with my boss. Anyone who has worked in a start-up will tell you that things change all the time, and impromptu meetings are a regular occurrence. But this meeting was different. As I sat huddled over my coffee on that bright August morning, my boss shared that our company was about to go through a restructure. She explained the reasons this was happening and then provided me with an ultimatum: as part of the restructure, they'd earmarked a new role for me, one that would come with a bigger team, more responsibility, and a more influential position in the company. But as my current role was being made redundant, if I didn't want to accept the new position, I'd have to leave the company. It would be my decision, and I had a week to think about it before confirming whether I'd stay or go.

You might think the decision would have been clear and straightforward to me. Surely I'd take the new job, right? The one that came with more power, more opportunities, and more responsibility. My ego definitely thought so—in fact, it was working overtime to convince me that there was no decision to make, that I should accept the new job and get stuck in. But a deeper, more authentic part of me wasn't quite sure. Call it my intuition. I'd spent all this time thinking about joy, exploring how I could invite more of it into my life. Surely, I thought, climbing further up the ladder in a career I knew deep down was wrong for me would get in the way of that?

In the end, it was checking in with my values that helped me to decide. I listed them out—freedom, connection, creativity, joy, security, and making an impact—and I weighed the two options against them. Accepting the bigger job would make my ego happy. I'd get to brag about my promotion on LinkedIn and Instagram and to my friends and colleagues. But it would take me further away from my values. I'd be working longer hours and sacrificing what little freedom I had left. I'd be moving into a more strategic role and away from being hands-on with my team—the work that I loved the most and the work that helped me to feel connected and like I was making an impact. Leaving the company and taking a gamble on this new thing I'd begun exploring struck fear into my heart (real, palpable fear, that flooded through me with many, many tears). But it was the option that felt most aligned with my values. The option that helped me to be creative and gain a sense of freedom. The option that put joy front and centre in my own life.

In the end, I decided to take the leap. It wasn't an easy decision to make. We didn't have a huge amount of savings to fall back on, and I spent the majority of my three-month notice period worrying about how we'd pay our mortgage. But I knew that if I took the promotion, once the ego buzz had worn off, I'd be left with a life that massively conflicted with my values and all of the challenges that came with that. Instead, I chose the route that, although difficult and scary, promised a better chance of joy in the long-term. It was a decision that confused my friends, family, and peers, but because I'd considered my values, I knew with conviction that it was the right decision for me. Three years later, I don't regret it.

LET'S RECAP

✳ All of us have a set of core values that shape us, even if we aren't yet aware of them.

✳ When we live life out of alignment with our values, we experience a sense of conflict that can manifest as comparison, stress, lack of motivation, and poor mental and physical health.

✳ Knowing our values can provide useful information in building a joyful life. They can act as a map, highlighting the changes we need to make to feel more aligned. We can also use them to help us make decisions that feel authentic and rewarding to us.

TWO

FIND YOUR PURPOSE & JOY

CHAPTER 4

THE FOUNDA

TIONS OF JO

UNPACKING THE SCIENCE OF WELL-BEING

In the last few years, thanks to the inimitable organising consultant Marie Kondo, a new phrase has entered our lexicon: spark joy. "Does this spark joy?" Kondo asks as she helps her clients decide which of their belongings to keep and which to get rid of, and it seems like over time, we've begun to apply the question to more than just our material possessions.

"Does this spark joy?" is a useful question to ask ourselves on our quest to build a more joyful life, but it can be a tricky one, too. How do you answer it if you haven't the foggiest idea what joy feels like? How do you answer it when you're struggling to list even a couple of things that bring you joy?

That might sound extreme, but it's the position that many of my clients find themselves in. They come to me convinced about the benefits of joy and determined to invite more of it into their lives, but they're always stuck on one question: how do I figure out what will bring me joy?

And that question always resonates with me because it's the question that swirled around my mind as I set off on my own joy journey. I knew I couldn't go on living in a way that felt so inauthentic to me, and I could talk for hours about the things that didn't bring me joy, but when it came to figuring out what did, I was stuck. Such a simple question felt like a riddle.

Often when clients admit that they don't know what would bring them joy, that they don't feel connected to the word or emotion, that they can't remember the last time they experienced it, they feel embarrassed. They see it as a sign that something must be wrong with them, or as a confirmation that they missed some fundamental lesson when they were growing up. What I always tell them, what I'll tell you now, what I wish someone had been able to tell me all those years ago, is this: there's nothing wrong with you; rather, there's something wrong with the structures, systems, and societies we are raised within.

Very few of us are ever encouraged to think about what will make us happiest or to consider what decisions or choices will spark joy for us. We see the quotes illustrated beautifully on Instagram or emblazoned on tote bags and notebooks: DO WHAT YOU LOVE! CHASE YOUR DREAMS! KEEP CHOOSING JOY! But nobody ever teaches us *how* to do that. Instead, we're taught how to fit into the system, how to play the game, how to be "successful" in the most socially acceptable definition of the word. We're taught to look to others for direction—to our parents or guardians, to our teachers, to our community leaders, to our bosses. We're taught that joy and happiness can be delayed until a later date, something to be enjoyed once we've worked hard enough or reached all of the milestones or proven ourselves to be exceptional.

It's little wonder, then, that when we start to consider what would bring us more joy, we hit a blank. It's little wonder that after years, decades even, of trying to follow everyone else's plan, we feel uncertain or unsure when it comes to figuring out the next steps for ourselves. That unmoored, disoriented feeling you might get when you think about joy isn't a sign that you're doing something wrong—it's simply a sign that this is new, and that's a good thing. When something is new, there's room for change, growth, and improvement.

Yet, I know that it might not feel that way to you right now, just as I know it doesn't always feel that way to my clients when I offer them those words of reassurance. I know, because six or seven years ago, I didn't feel optimistic. I felt lost. I'd started to untether myself from the belief system I'd built my whole life around. I'd spent my first twenty-six years on Earth believing that if I just made all of the "right" decisions, if I just played by society's rules, I'd be happy, and suddenly I knew with glittering clarity that this belief wasn't true. But I didn't yet have anything else to replace that belief system with. I'd spent my whole life striving for the next thing, and now, without the confidence that achieving the next milestone would make me happy, I didn't know where to direct my energy.

If you're feeling the same way, I want to assure you that things can change. While there's no one-size-fits-all approach to finding and prioritising joy, there are tools, ideas, and research findings to get you started. We'll spend the next few chapters exploring them. And the good news is that choosing joy is like exercising a muscle. The more you do it, the easier it will become.

CHOOSING JOY IS LIKE EXERCISING A MUSCLE. THE MORE YOU DO IT, THE EASIER IT WILL BECOME.

The Foundations Of Joy

When it comes to understanding what might add more joy to our lives, the field of positive psychology is a great place to start. Positive psychology is sometimes colloquially referred to as the science of making things better, and since it was first recognised as a formal domain of psychology back in 2000, scientists have undertaken research to understand the science of well-being, flourishing, and positive emotions.

Like most research fields, positive psychology isn't without its pitfalls. One key criticism is that a vast majority of studies in this domain have relied on populations that can be categorised as WEIRD, meaning that research participants come from Western, educated, industrialised, rich, and democratic backgrounds (Hendriks et al. 2018, 489-501). In the past few years, the field has acknowledged and endeavoured to change this lack of inclusivity, with new studies taking care to recruit participants from a more diverse range of backgrounds. But it's important to note that, as with any scientific findings, we can't assume that the same approach will work for everyone.

We are all unique individuals, with different perspectives, experiences, and needs. There's no checklist when it comes to joy, no ten-point programme to help you build your most joyful life. But some of the findings from positive psychology can provide a useful starting point as we begin to explore what will spark joy for each of us. Let's dig into some of those findings.

Connection

When it comes to joy and happiness, the research is clear: connection is key. In fact, one major Harvard study following more than seven hundred men over the course of their lives found that those who were more socially connected to their family, friends, and communities were the happiest, healthiest, and most resilient (Mineo 2017). The study highlighted that the quality of the participants' close relationships was a greater indicator of happiness and joy than income, class, IQ, or even genes.

Important to note is that researchers found that these relationships don't have to be perfect. We can bicker and argue with our closest connections, but as long as we still feel that we can count on them when times are hard, we'll reap the benefits that close relationships can bring.

In summary, if we're looking to add more joy to our lives, a good place to start is by investing in our relationships and ensuring that we feel connected to the people around us.

Experiences Over Things

If you were to look at your monthly outgoings, would you say you're spending more money on experiences or things? Fancy advertising campaigns can make us believe that buying new things will make us happier, but the research shows that we get more joy for our buck if we invest in experiences instead (University of Texas at Austin 2020).

There are a few reasons for this. Firstly, we get used to new possessions quickly. You might have experienced this when buying a new phone, for example. For the first couple of days, you're excited by all of its features and how much better the camera is, and yet, within a couple of weeks, the novelty has already worn off. Another factor is that possessions can often lead to comparison. You might buy a new car and be thrilled with it, until your neighbour buys a better one. In short, we overestimate how much joy buying something new will bring us, and even if we do experience a surge of joy upon making the purchase, that joy tends to be short-lived.

Experiences, on the other hand, seem to be a better investment in our joy. For one thing, when we spend our money on something experiential, we get the bonus of anticipation—that glorious feeling of looking forward to a meal out or an upcoming trip. In addition, experiences last in recollection. Once your new iPhone stops working, you'll recycle it and never think about it again, whereas the memories of dancing to your favourite band at a music festival or watching the sunset on a family vacation will persist over time.

Savouring

Sometimes referred to as "the art of noticing," savouring is all about getting the most out of your positive experiences. It's easy to assume that when good things happen, we automatically experience joy, but research shows that we don't always maximise the effects of positive experiences. Savouring occurs when we are mindfully engaged, or as researcher Fred Bryant puts it, "It is like swishing the experience around in your mind" (Kennelly 2012).

There are a few ways we can practise savouring in our day-to-day. Sharing good news with others or reflecting on your positive experiences are good places to start. Also, allowing yourself to be fully present in the moment, perhaps by practising meditation or mindfulness, can empower you to take in the beauty of the here and now. Or take a "mental photograph," pausing for a moment to take stock of what you want to remember from the moment.

Moving

Before I dive into this topic, I wanted to acknowledge that there's a lot of privilege involved in being able to move our bodies freely. If physical activity isn't possible for you, or if this section feels unhelpful in any way, please feel free to skip it.

We all know that exercise is good for our physical health, but an abundance of research shows it can boost our mental health, too. There are several ideas about why physical activity can make us feel so good, over and above our understanding that exercise encourages the release of positive endorphins (Huppert et al. 2005). One theory is that physical activity provides a distraction from the stresses of everyday life, while another suggests that it can make us feel more in control, thus boosting our self-worth and self-esteem. Yet another claims that committing to regular exercise or movement can change the way we view ourselves and allow us to experience personal growth, which in turn brings us a sense of joy and contentment.

Further research shows that the benefits of physical activity are greater if undertaken in blue or green spaces, spaces abundant in nature. I've found this to be true in my own life—while a good gym workout will get those positive endorphins flowing, a gentle hike in the countryside feels much more joyful.

Practising Kindness

Robust research shows that people who are inclined to be kind and charitable report being happier and experiencing more positive emotions (Lyubomirsky, Sonja and King 2005, 803-855). In fact, one study found that performing just one act of kindness a week was associated with an increase in well-being compared to a control group.

While research on what acts of kindness or volunteer activities boost our moods most significantly is still thin on the ground, it appears that there's greater benefit to engaging in activities within a community setting. The likely reason is that we receive an extra boost that comes from an enhanced social life and the feeling that we belong.

Lifelong Learning

You might think that learning stops when you leave school, but there's evidence to suggest that possessing the curiosity of a lifelong learner can help us to access more joy. Learning something new helps us to feel accomplished, which can create positive emotions. Researchers have also found that we can only enter flow states (a sense of being in the zone and immersed in a feeling of energised focus known to produce intense feelings of enjoyment) when we are working on something with an adequate level of challenge.

Just as the benefits of practising kindness are greater in a community setting, researchers believe that the benefits of learning can be even greater when we share those learning experiences with others, either by learning in a group environment, or by sharing new skills or findings with our loved ones or wider community.

Creativity

Finally, studies suggest that there's a strong link between how much time we spend being creative and our sense of well-being and flourishing (Conner et al. 2016, 181-189). Engaging our creativity is also thought to boost our positive emotions, giving us a greater chance of experiencing joy.

Sometimes we label ourselves as "not the creative type," but research shows that creativity can be fostered in anyone. It doesn't just mean picking up a paintbrush or attending a figure-drawing class—dancing, playing an instrument, taking photographs, or even applying a creative approach to problem-solving can flex the muscle! How often do you engage in creative activities?

Look For The Signs

We can use these foundational elements of joy and well-being as a jumping-off point to spark ideas that might add more joy to our lives. The following prompts, questions, and ideas will guide you in that effort. Though I've included a wide variety of ideas here, the aim isn't to try them all! Instead, choose the ones that feel most appealing or interesting to you and give them a go. Start small and trust yourself—these are jumping off points rather than written rules, so if something doesn't feel good to you, leave it. Trust your intuition!

Connection

→ Think about a typical week in your life. How much time do you spend with your closest loved ones? Does this feel like enough time?

→ What changes could you make to carve out more time for your friends and family?

→ Brainstorm different ways you could feel connected to your loved ones, even if it's difficult to be with them in person. Here are some ideas: send them a handwritten letter, set up a regular virtual coffee date, or print photos of special memories to display in your home.

→ Arrange a time to meet up with friends or family and treat it as a priority.

→ Reach out to someone you have lost touch with and let them know you're thinking about them.

Experiences Over Things

→ Dig out a recent bank statement and calculate the split of spending between material items (essential items not included) and experiences. What does the balance look like?

→ Write about a time you saved up to buy a material item. How did you feel when you bought it? Did it bring you as much joy as you hoped in the long-term?

→ Write about a time you saved up to buy an experience. How did you feel when you bought it? Did it bring you as much joy as you hoped in the long-term?

→ Make a list of things you'd love to experience in the next few years and start to plan how you can check each item off.

→ Set up a savings pot specifically for the experiences you'd love to have and add to it whenever you can.

→ Consider asking loved ones for experiences or vouchers for experiences as gifts instead of material items.

Savouring

→ Look around you and describe your current surroundings. What can you see, hear, taste, smell, and feel in this present moment?

→ Write about a moment you will never forget, in as much detail as you can remember. What happened? How did you feel?

→ Head out for an "awe walk," a stroll during which you intentionally shift your attention outwards instead of inwards. Pay attention to all of the beauty you can see on your walk, noticing how you feel.

→ As you move through your day, try to take some "mental photographs." Which parts of your day do you most want to remember?

→ Identify a part of your day that you'd like to consciously savour. Try to be fully present during those moments, noticing how it changes your experience.

Moving

→ Make a playlist of all of your favourite songs and have a little dance party at home.

→ Think about how you used to move and play as a child. Does reflecting on this spark any ideas about how you could invite more movement into your day-to-day life?

→ Research green or blue spaces where you could walk, jog, paddle, or swim.

→ Let go of what you know and give yourself permission to move for fun. It's not about how many calories you burn; it's about feeling connected to your body in a joyful way.

→ Think about how you could add a small amount of movement to your day. Even a ten-minute walk at lunchtime can make a huge difference!

Practising Kindness

→ Make a list of all the ways you could spread some kindness to others, and then commit to ticking off one item each week.

→ Think about how you can practise more kindness in your day-to-day life. How could you be kinder to your family members, work colleagues, and friends?

→ Explore opportunities to volunteer in your area.

→ Give someone a genuine compliment or write a heartfelt thank you note the next time you receive great customer service.

→ Practise a loving kindness meditation to show yourself some of the same compassion you show to others.

Lifelong Learning

→ Write about a time you've persevered to learn something new. What did you learn about yourself in the process?

→ Reflect on who you were this time last year. What have you learned since then?

→ Write a list of things you'd love to learn during your lifetime. What are you curious about? What skills would you love to have? Then determine a place to start.

→ Identify something you'd love to learn just for the fun of it, rather than something to further your career.

→ Do you have any skills that you could teach to others?

Creativity

→ Make a list of creative activities you used to love to engage in as a child. Does reflecting on this spark any ideas about how you could invite more creativity into your day-to-day life?

→ Take a task from your to-do list and consider what would be the most creative way to complete it. Commit to trying a creative activity you've never experienced before. Book a class, find a YouTube video, or ask a friend to help you get started.

→ Challenge yourself to create something from scratch. You could write a poem, draw something, or bake a cake. Try to focus on the process rather than the outcome.

→ Fill your creative-inspiration cup. Reread a favourite book, listen to a classic album, or go to a museum or art gallery.

REALITY CHECK JOY

In this chapter, I've shared a lot of information about the foundations of joy, and if you're not currently engaging with these foundations, it can be overwhelming to know where to begin. But remember that you don't need to go from zero to one hundred overnight. Even the slightest shift in the direction of joy will make a big impact. Choose the foundation that feels most inviting to you, then get started.

For an extra serving of joy, consider how you can combine one or more of the foundations of joy. For example, could you flex your creativity by learning something new at an art class, and get a little boost of connection by inviting your friend along? Could you practise savouring nature by exercising in a blue or green space?

LET'S RECAP

✳   There's no one-size-fits-all approach when it comes to joy, but the research suggests that there are some foundational elements that can provide a good jumping-off point.

✳   The core foundations of joy include:

   o   Connection
   o   Prioritising experiences over things
   o   Savouring
   o   Moving
   o   Practising kindness
   o   Committing to lifelong learning
   o   Exploring creativity

✳   Planning some activities in each of these areas can help us start to add more joy to our lives.

FOLLOW THE CLUES

CHAPTER 5

LEANING INTO WHAT FEELS GOOD

Now that we've explored some of the foundations of joy, hopefully you have some ideas about what you can do to invite a little more joy into your life. It can feel exciting to start making plans and realising them, but remember that joy doesn't require perfection or ambitious goals. In fact, often the best way to start adding more joy to our lives is by listening to the clues our bodies and brains give us and starting small.

When I committed to building a more joyful life for myself, I relied on a mantra. I repeated it to myself over and over again, I wrote it in my journal, and I came back to it whenever I was feeling wobbly. Despite being only five words, over time, it changed my life completely: *Lean into what feels good.*

It sounds simple, and it is, really. But so few of us give ourselves permission to lean into what feels good. We've been taught that the things worth having are supposed to be hard. We've been taught that we need to hustle, to stretch ourselves thin, to do everything we can to fulfil our potential. We've been taught that the "happily ever after" lies on the other side of all that effort, rather than in the present, so we deny ourselves the things that feel good right now in the hope that we'll get to experience that joy later.

But now is all we have. You're allowed to feel good *now*. You're allowed to choose ease and fun and joy and peace right here, right now. To begin with, it might feel uncomfortable, unfamiliar, but by leaning into what feels good, you'll be choosing joy. By listening to those little clues that your mind and body are trying to give you, feeling good will become your norm, and in time, so will choosing joy.

It's okay to start very small. When I first started using that mantra, the shifts in my day-to-day life were almost imperceptible. Leaning into what felt good looked like waking up ten minutes later. It looked like making myself a breakfast that I was excited to eat, instead of forcing myself to eat what I thought I should. It looked like getting outside for five minutes of fresh air during my lunch hour. It looked like picking up a juicy novel, instead of watching an episode of a TV show I wasn't even enjoying that much. These were small shifts rather than huge life changes, but they were life-changing in their power. Because every time I leant into what felt good, I was choosing a little sliver of joy, and I was building the muscle of putting myself first. In time, that muscle strengthened, and before long, I was thinking about how I could lean into what felt good in all areas of my life—from my work to my relationships, from my health to my hobbies.

The Role Of Gratitude

A useful tool to start noticing what feels good is gratitude, which has so many other benefits, too. In fact, studies show that gratitude is a vital ingredient for living a joyful life.

Gratitude has several definitions in positive psychology research, but the one I like the most comes from Sansone & Sansone (2010), who write that "With gratitude, people acknowledge the goodness in their lives." In this sense, gratitude is an art in noticing and celebrating what is already good, instead of directing all of our energy into what we'd like to change or what could be better. It's about celebrating the way our lives are right now, instead of comparing ourselves to others and feeling bad as a result.

Gratitude has been shown to improve our physical health, increase prosocial behaviour, help us to cultivate resilience, and protect against burnout (Sansone and Sansone 2010). Most pertinent to our topic is the link between gratitude and joy: it appears you can't have one without the other. Researcher Brené Brown has said that in her twelve years of research, gathering over 11,000 pieces of data, she didn't interview a single person who identified as joyful who didn't have a regular gratitude practice (Brown 2018). When I first read that research had proven joy and gratitude to be linked, I thought it was obvious. When you have a joyful life, you're grateful for it, right? It made sense to me to think of it that way, but it turns out that I'd gotten my cause and effect the wrong way round. Brown's work has shown that people aren't grateful because of their joyful lives—they have joyful lives because they're grateful.

This was certainly my experience. In fact, without gratitude, I wouldn't have even gotten started on my joy journey. Back in 2016, just after my cousin had passed away, life felt very bleak. Mustering up any sense of positivity felt impossible. I'd just lost someone so very important to me, and my entire family, the people I'm closest to, were heartbroken and grieving. When I thought about the future, it felt incredibly difficult to picture. I'd lost faith in everything I thought I knew about the world, and hope felt very, very far away. Back then, I would have found it hard to focus on those foundational elements of joy we explored in the last chapter. Simply making it through the day took all of my energy and moving my body or trying to learn something new would have felt completely out of the question. But what I could do, even amongst all of the grief and sadness and trauma and tears, was practise gratitude.

That gratitude manifested in many ways. I remember feeling so thankful for the kind neighbours who left plates of sandwiches on the doorstep on the morning of Blossom's funeral, because they knew that otherwise we might not have eaten. I remember feeling abundantly grateful for my partner and for the close ties we had with our family—we never once felt alone. I had so much appreciation for my colleagues who picked up my workload and ensured I wouldn't have to worry about emails going unanswered, for our friends who rallied around us and showed us so much love, for the simple things that provided some much-needed levity: a sunny morning, a kind text, a smile from a stranger. Even amid that heavy grief, gratitude could still exist.

And those small doses of gratitude were incredibly powerful. They fortified me. They built my resilience. They made me stronger. They gave me the courage to keep putting one foot in front of the other. And in time, those moments of gratitude helped me to reconnect to joy. By noticing the things that I felt most grateful for, I was able to experience those first small sparks of pleasure after weeks spent under a heavy cloud. By feeling the full weight of my appreciation for what I did have, I was able to recognise the fresh bursts of contentment pushing through what I'd assumed was barren ground. And as the weeks and months rolled by, these sparks and roots helped me to start to put my life back together in a way that felt more joyful, more authentic, and more meaningful than it had before.

Gratitude helped me to gently navigate my way out of a traumatic and difficult time, but you don't have to experience some sort of tragedy for gratitude to be useful. I believe that practising more thankfulness and appreciation can be transformative for us all. And it can also give us useful information when it comes to building a joyful life. By taking time to notice what we're grateful for, we not only get to feel the good feelings that come with reliving special moments or appreciating all that we have, but we also start to notice what's most important to us. That in turn can help us determine where to put more focus on the path to inviting more joy into our lives. It helps us to build a stronger relationship with our intuition, to nurture the things our bodies and minds want more of, and to build a sense of how we want our lives to look that isn't informed by advertising or the expectations of others.

Put simply, gratitude is an incredible tool when it comes to finding joy. It's a tool that has played a pivotal role in my own life, and something that I recommend in abundance to all of my clients. But just because we know something works doesn't always mean that it's easy to put into practise. Sometimes, the stresses of life take over, and we become so busy focusing on and planning for the big, extraordinary, future moments, that we forget to feel grateful for all that we have right now.

I'm not immune to this myself. A couple of months ago, I was out jogging in my local area. I'd forced myself away from my desk (because I know how important movement is for my own joy) and as I was shuffling along, putting one foot in front of the other, my mind was preoccupied. I was thinking about our upcoming vacation, mentally replaying my to-do list in my mind, and wondering if I'd have time to squeeze it all in. I was worrying about a project I had on at work, brainstorming ways I could ensure it was a success. I was thinking about what I was going to wear for my friend's birthday drinks and wondering whether or not she'd like the gift I'd bought her. My physical body was there, jogging along the river, but my mind was stretched in several other places.

About halfway into my jog, I passed an older gentleman out for a walk. He stopped and turned to me, arms outstretched to the sky, and said cheerfully, "Aren't we lucky to be having such a beautiful day?" Joy burst from his smile, and I could tell that he was totally rooted in the moment, feeling the warmth of the sun on his skin and taking in the blossoms unfurling all around us. I, on the other hand, had barely even registered the weather that morning, so preoccupied I was with everything else running through my mind. I was missing out on the joy right in front of me by worrying about a future that hadn't even happened yet.

That experience taught me a lesson. When we focus too much on those big, milestone moments, we often forget to enjoy all of the little moments that make a life. Joyful moments needn't be saved solely for holidays and birthdays. Gratitude is a process that helps us to ground ourselves in the here and now so that we can soak up all of the joy on offer every day. It might feel hard to prioritise sometimes, but it's always worth it.

When Finding Gratitude Feels Difficult

What if practising gratitude feels hard? So often when I'm working with clients, they'll tell me that they know they should feel grateful, that they know on paper they have a "good" life, but that they're struggling to *feel* gratitude for it.

This might feel true for you, too. Perhaps you feel that you *should* feel grateful for your job and the income that it provides you, but deep down all you feel is a sense of dissatisfaction. Perhaps you feel that you *should* feel grateful for your home and the security you have, but really, you're itching for a big adventure somewhere new. Perhaps you feel that you *should* feel grateful for your supportive partner, but you can't quite shake the feeling that you might be happier on your own.

If that resonates, if you find yourself struggling to practise gratitude even though you have something that other people tell you that you should be grateful for, let's look at it from a different perspective. Firstly, take a moment to show yourself heaps of compassion. Struggling to practise gratitude doesn't make you a bad person; it doesn't make you spoiled or unappreciative. It's simply a sign that something isn't right. Next, listen to what that lack of gratitude is trying to teach you, and trust yourself. If you struggle to feel grateful for some aspect of your life despite its supposed benefits, that's a sign that something needs to change. In fact, this can be a great way to figure out what might add more joy to your life. If you're struggling to feel grateful for your job, there might be a more joyful work situation out there for you. If you're struggling to feel grateful for your home and the security you have, changing things up might spark some joy. If you're struggling to feel grateful for your partner, consider shifts you could make that would make you feel more joyful in the long run. You get the picture.

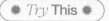
 Try This

There's no one way to practise gratitude, but here are some tried and tested questions that I use with clients that help to tune into and feel appreciative for the best bits of your life. As always, I invite you to use them in whatever way feels best to you.

- Who are the people you are most grateful for in your life? What do they bring to your life?

- What aspects of your life would your ancestors be most jealous of? What privileges do you have today that they would have loved to have?

- Consider where you live. What do you love most about it? If a tourist arrived in your town or city, what would they be excited about?

- List five things that you miss from your everyday life when you're away on holiday. How could you start to value these things more every day?

- How is your life more positive today than it was a year ago?

- What is your favourite thing about the season we are currently experiencing?

- Think about the different days of the week. What is your favourite thing about each day? (Yes, even Monday!)

- What freedoms are you most grateful for?

- Think about some of the more difficult or challenging periods of your life and reconsider them from a place of gratitude. What did they teach you about yourself? What positives did those situations bring into your life?

- Think back to who you were five years ago. How has your life changed for the better since then? What would the version of you from five years ago make of your current life?

Changing The Perspective

Cognitive reframing, an effort to change the perspective or lens through which you view a certain situation, is a helpful tool to put gratitude into action during difficult times.

Here's an example from my own life: a couple of years ago, my husband and I were awoken on a Saturday morning by our neighbour knocking loudly on our front door. She was calling to let us know that a pipe had burst in our garden, and water was gushing out of our gate, right down the street.

Now this would have been an annoying thing to happen on any day, but my husband and I had been due to head away for a weekend by the seaside. I'd spent the whole week dreaming of long walks on the beach, relaxing by the fire with a good book, and generally recharging after a busy couple of months. Within ten minutes of that knock on our door, we realised that our trip wasn't going to be possible, and on top of that, we were about to be stung with a hefty call-out fee for an emergency plumber.

It would have been so easy to spend the whole weekend moping and feeling sorry for ourselves, to let the burst pipe and the cancelled trip be a catalyst for all sorts of misery. But instead, we practised some cognitive reframing. Just a few years previously, we had been desperate to have the comfort and security of our own home, and we were so grateful to have finally met that goal, even if it meant having to deal with an emergency every now and then. We could feel grateful that the pipe had burst when we had a little bit of money stowed away for emergencies, something that hadn't always been the case. And even though our weekend hadn't exactly gone to plan, we still got to spend time together, and we even managed a little chuckle at the situation once our initial worries had worn off.

Cognitive reframing isn't the same as toxic positivity. It's not about denying the negative emotions we might feel. Instead, it's about minimising the impact they have on us. Spending a few minutes searching for the good and finding things to feel grateful for despite the inconvenience changed our reactions to the situation. We bounced back quickly and still got to enjoy our weekend, which wouldn't have been possible without a quick reframe.

Using What You Know

Another way to start hunting out your joy clues is by using what you already know. In Part One, we touched on tools that we're going to use to help us do just that. If you don't already have them to hand, now is the time to dig out your joy wheel and your list of values.

Let's start with the joy wheel. As we discussed in Chapter Two, your completed joy wheel gives us a snapshot of how your life is currently feeling. Now, we'll use that information to help us think about the changes that will make a positive difference.

First, take each of the spokes/areas of life, considering them one at a time, and imagine what would have to be different for you to score at ten out of ten. Give yourself permission to think big here. To be fully satisfied in each area of your life, what would that look like? This will give us clues about what the most joyful version of your life would look like.

Once you've thought about that, revisit each spoke and try to define a small change you could start making now that could improve your score by one or two points. This will form a list of actions you can start to take in the short term to add a little joy to your life.

Once you've done that, complete the same steps, but this time revisit your values. Again, ask yourself what would have to change to feel completely aligned to each value, and what action you could start taking immediately to help you feel more aligned in the short term.

After completing these exercises, you should have a clearer and more authentic picture of what the most joyful version of your life would look like, supported by mini actions you can take right now to add more joy to your everyday life.

Permission To Dream

To build a truly joyful life, you need to give yourself permission to dream. So often I see people close the door on their hopes and dreams before they've even fully explored them. I understand why—it can be tricky to dream of something better when we've spent so long living a less than joyful existence. And I'm not saying that it's always possible to create your dream life overnight, sometimes there are tangible things you might need to work through to bring your hopes and ambitions into existence.

But when we cut ourselves off in the dreaming stage, when we prevent ourselves from even exploring what would truly feel good to us, we hinder our own ability to understand what would bring us more joy. We cut ourselves off from the possibility of optimism, and instead we stay rooted in cynicism.

You don't need to know how you'll bring your most joyful life to fruition right now (we'll spend the whole of Section Three diving into that), but you do need to allow yourself to picture it. So, as you work through these exercises and start to picture what the most joyful and aligned version of your life would look like, try to hold back those limiting thoughts telling you that it isn't possible. You can acknowledge those thoughts, you can even jot them down somewhere if that helps, but don't take them as fact. A more joyful life is possible for you, and the first step to building it is imagining it.

✦ A Sprinkle OF JOY ✦

For inspiration for clarifying your vision of the future, the following exercise might help. It's called Best Possible Self, and it comes from a piece of research conducted by Dr. Laura King in 2001 (in 2001, 798-807). King's research found that writing about our best possible future selves can boost hope, improve our well-being, and help us to build a more optimistic mindset. My own research completed back in 2021 found that the Best Possible Self tool helped people to find more clarity when exploring career goals.

Let's dive in. Here is the prompt used in Dr. King's pilot study:

Think about your life in the future. Imagine that everything has gone as well as it possibly could. You have worked hard and succeeded at accomplishing all of your life goals. Think of this as the realisation of all of your life dreams. Now, write about what you imagined. The instructions from the original study invited participants to write about what they had imagined for twenty minutes, then to repeat the exercise on four consecutive days. However, there is evidence to suggest that the exercise is useful even if only completed once or twice.

LET'S RECAP

✳ Inviting more joy into our lives doesn't always mean making big, grand changes. Sometimes it can be as simple as leaning into what feels good.

✳ Gratitude is a great way to notice what feels good in our lives, in addition to plenty of other benefits, including improving health, increasing prosocial behaviour, cultivating resilience, and protecting against burnout. Gratitude and joy are intrinsically linked.

✳ We can also add more joy to our lives by using what we already know is and isn't working. The joy wheel and values exercise can help us to do this.

✳ An important part of identifying joy is suspending disbelief and allowing ourselves to dream.

the power of purpose

DISCOVERING YOUR SPARK

When it comes to figuring out what sparks joy, there's one last important area to explore: purpose. Purpose has become a buzzword in the last few years, especially in relation to our careers. The media often publishes articles and essays about how we're all quitting our jobs and chasing our purpose. But what do we mean by purpose? It can sometimes feel like an intangible concept—something that we're all supposed to want but can't quite pin down.

So, let's start by looking at the official definition from the research. According to *Greater Good Magazine*, psychologists define purpose as "an abiding intention to achieve a long-term goal that is both personally meaningful and makes a positive mark on the world" (Greater Good Magazine, n.d.). There are a few key elements to unpack in that definition. Firstly, purpose involves intention: we're actively choosing where we want to put our energy and focus. Secondly, it's about working towards a long-term goal: our purpose is usually something that can drive us over a long period of time (or even our entire lives), as opposed to a short-term objective. And finally, our purpose will be both personally meaningful and make a positive impact on the world: it lies at the intersection of providing satisfaction and meaning for us as individuals and contributing to something beyond us.

I like to think of purpose as our "why." It's the driving force behind what we do, it's the reason we keep on going even when times get tough, and it's what feels important to us when we think about the meaning of life. When we figure out our purpose and start to live in a way that aligns with that purpose, there are a whole host of benefits in store for us.

First, many psychological benefits are associated with having a sense of purpose, including a greater sense of self-esteem and confidence, improved psychological well-being, increased life satisfaction, and a greater capacity for dealing with stress (John Templeton Foundation 2022). Physical benefits are plentiful, too—one study showed that cortisol levels tend to be lower in people engaged in purposeful living, which is significant because higher levels of stress hormones are associated with a whole variety of health issues. And finally, having a sense of purpose can improve our chances of success, because it increases our levels of resilience, grit, and intrinsic motivation. In a nutshell, purpose is a vital ingredient for joy, and it benefits just about every area of our lives.

As with other aspects of a joyful life we've discussed, having a sense of purpose isn't a magical fix-all, but it can be a powerful tool. Finding my own purpose has had such an impact on my own sense of joy and contentment that I wanted to dedicate a chapter to it. When I think back to some of those early career experiences, the ones that left me feeling as though something major was missing, I've since realised that I lacked a sense of purpose. I was good at the work I did, I was rewarded well for it, and I received plenty of praise and recognition, but the issue was that I didn't truly care about the work I was doing. It didn't feel like work I'd intentionally chosen, I didn't possess a long-term goal, and I certainly didn't feel as though I was working on something that was personally meaningful or having a positive impact on the world.

When I decided to leave my corporate career behind and strike out on my own, building a business from scratch, things were certainly not plain sailing. I didn't have a huge amount of savings behind me (nowhere near the six months' salary often recommended before leaving a job). I was walking away from all of the benefits I'd become accustomed to and into an uncertain future. I didn't even have a detailed business strategy to guide my next steps. I was taking a huge gamble, and one that wasn't just risky for me, but for my husband, too. Having always been the breadwinner in our marriage, walking away from the security of corporate employment felt like rolling the dice on the life and home we'd built together.

One thing I did have, though—one thing I'd never had in my arsenal be-fore—was a strong sense of purpose. I had a clear and compelling "why"—I wanted to help people live their most joyful lives, whatever that meant to them, and I was determined to spread the message of joy as far and wide as I possibly could. It was clinging on to this sense of purpose that helped me to weather the knocks that came my way in those first few months. It was understanding my "why" that helped me to keep showing up despite the inevitable rejections or the difficulty in managing my business finances for the first time.

But I don't think that sense of purpose was ever more vital for me than when the pandemic hit in March 2020. I was only in my fourth month of self-em-ployment, and I was still very much finding my feet as a new business owner, when suddenly we were all confined to our homes, and the economy rolled to a standstill. While friends and ex-colleagues were furloughed or offered support and reassurance from their employers, I lost huge swathes of work overnight—events were cancelled, clients pulled out of contracts, brand partners went silent.

It would have been so easy to quit at that moment. To see this as a sign from the universe that this wasn't the right move for me, to find a new job that would offer me some security amid all of the uncertainty. But, despite all of the worry and anxiety and tears—and believe me, there were many tears!—that strong sense of purpose kept me going. I had no idea what path lay ahead, but knowing and understanding my "why" provided the direction I needed to keep putting one foot in front of the other and figuring out the next step as I went. The world had changed and some of my goals and plans had to change as a result, but my purpose never did. It was my steady and constant North Star as I navigated those choppy waters.

From that experience, I learned that life very rarely goes according to plan. That can feel scary and overwhelming, but having a sense of purpose keeps us afloat during those tricky times. Not only did knowing my purpose help me to keep showing up from a business perspective, it was also so important for my mental and emotional stamina. It gave me a sense of meaning when so many other areas of my life were cut off. It helped me to build resilience, knowing I could make it through the hard times. And most importantly, living my purpose brought me a huge amount of joy. But I'm not the only one who experienced these benefits. Research published in 2021 found that having a life purpose reduced loneliness and countered some of the negative impacts of stress during the COVID-19 pandemic (Kang et al., 2021).

✦ A Sprinkle OF JOY ✦

Think about a time when your life felt most purposeful. What was happening? How were you spending your time? How did living with purpose make you feel? These reflections can help you to uncover more clues about what will bring you joy.

A Tool To Help You Find Your Purpose

Now that we understand the importance of purpose, how do we go about figuring out our own purpose? That's a question I get asked a lot, and I understand why—it can sometimes feel a bit like looking for a needle in a haystack, difficult to know where or how to start. A tool that I use with my clients provides a useful framework for structuring your thoughts: the purpose map.

If the purpose map looks familiar to you, that's because it's been adapted from a Japanese concept called *ikigai*, meaning "reason for living." In the *ikigai* model, there are four overlapping circles, whereas I prefer to focus on just three: what you love, what you're good at, and what the world needs. The *ikigai* model also includes what you can be paid for. I choose not to include this for a couple of reasons: 1) Some of us might be searching for a sense of purpose outside of our careers and therefore needing to be paid isn't as important, and 2) If your purpose is something that the world needs, you're likely adding value that you can charge for if you so wish.

Our purpose map suggests that your purpose lies at the intersection of these three areas. Let's dive into each of them.

What You Love

The first section explores what you love—the things you enjoy most, whatever feels like the best parts of life to you. It can help to ask yourself what you're passionate about and what excites you, or even to revisit what you loved to do as a child. It might also be useful to revisit some of your answers from the values exercise in Chapter Three for some inspiration.

What You're Good At

Next, we look at what you're good at. This is where we want to focus on your strengths and your unique selling points, or the special bits that make you *you*. Often this is where my clients get stuck, because we're not very good at blowing our own trumpets, but we all have our own unique strengths. Think about what comes most naturally to you—are there certain tasks or activities that you find easy, despite others struggling with them? It can also be useful to reflect on positive feedback you've received or roles you tend to

WHAT YOU LOVE

Connection

Having an impact

Self-development

Freedom

WHAT YOU'RE GOOD AT

Listening

Helping people find answers

Building relationships

WHAT THE WORLD NEEDS

Confidence

A focus on happiness + joy

More positivity

PURPOSE

Helping people live their most joyful lives

fall into within your friendship groups. For example, if you're the one always planning the get-togethers, you might have a flair for organisation.

What the World Needs

The final section is where we turn outwards and think about the positive impact we want to have on the world. Try not to let the title of "what the world needs" overwhelm you. Sure, the world needs peace and a cure for cancer, but it also needs beautiful art and new ideas and fun experiences. It might help to ask yourself what problem you'd like to play a small role in helping to solve or alleviate. It doesn't matter how big an impact your purpose has, just that it's connected to something bigger than you.

Putting it All Together

Your purpose will be something that encompasses all three of these areas: something you enjoy, something you're good at, and something that has a positive impact on others. If it doesn't bring together all three sections, it's not your purpose. For example, lots of us do work that we're good at and that delivers something that the world needs, but if we don't enjoy it, it won't feel purposeful to us. Alternatively, you might have a brilliant idea that brings together your strengths and your passions, but if it isn't going to positively impact anyone but you, it's probably more of a hobby than a purpose.

Use the blank chart to the right to begin to map out your own purpose.

WHAT YOU LOVE

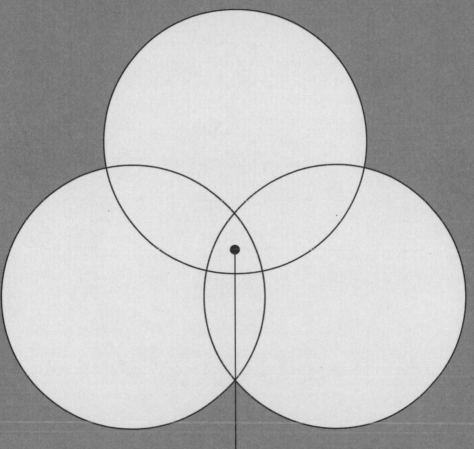

WHAT YOU'RE
GOOD AT

WHAT THE
WORLD NEEDS

PURPOSE

A Few Things To Bear In Mind

→ Purpose is personal. We'll each have a purpose that is unique to us, and there's no value in comparing your purpose to anybody else's. To reap the benefits of having a purpose, it needs to feel authentic to you, so focus on that and try to avoid the comparison trap.

→ It's okay if you don't know exactly what your purpose is yet, or if you feel you can't define it in a neat or concise way. Use the clues you have from exploring the three areas and get curious! Sometimes a bit of experimentation or conversation can offer a new perspective that can help you to figure it out.

→ You don't have to be an expert to live your purpose. Remember that purpose isn't about quickly achieving a goal; it's about working on something over a sustained period of time. It will feel much more enjoyable if your purpose creates an opportunity for you to grow and develop, instead of requiring perfection already.

Purposes aren't solely reserved for the world of work. Your purpose might be a side project you want to launch, a hobby you want to pursue deeper, a community project you want to be involved in, or something you'd love to do with your family. Try not to put too much pressure on yourself to turn your purpose into work if that doesn't feel right to you. And remember: it's okay to start small. You don't have to concentrate on your purpose for twenty-four hours a day to reap the benefits. In fact, having a purpose that drives you is so impactful that you'll experience more joy, even if you can only act on it for an hour or two a week.

When I first realised that my purpose was helping people to live more joyful lives, I didn't immediately quit my job. I didn't even rush off to retrain as a coach right away. Instead, I thought of little ways I could spread the message of joy in the hour or two I could spare each week.

I shared ideas and tips on Instagram. I started a podcast in which I shared fifteen-minute episodes on all things positivity. I wrote blog posts about navigating my own joy journey. Even without making any other changes to my life, putting my purpose into action for just an hour or two a week brought me so much joy, and it gave me the energy and confidence to make bigger changes down the line.

So, whatever your purpose might be, ask yourself this: What is the smallest possible way I can act on this today? Then, do that thing. Don't wait until you've gotten some big plan figured out. It's by taking action, even if it's small, that you'll feel the benefits and start to see what's possible.

Try This

Complete the following three sentences:

I love ____________________

I am great at ____________________

The world needs more ____________________

Then brainstorm some ways you can bring your answers to each prompt together.

Once you've figured out what lies at the intersection, consider the following questions and exercises:

- What excites you about your purpose?
- Make a list of all the different ways you could act on your purpose.
- Make a list of the people who might be able to help you put your purpose into action.
- Consider what would be the smallest action you could take. Then take it!

LET'S RECAP

✳ Purpose is defined as taking intentional action towards a long-term goal that is both personally meaningful and makes a positive mark on the world.

✳ Having a purpose can improve our health, boost our self-esteem, increase our chances of success, and enhance our life satisfaction. It can also help us to be more resilient during difficult times.

✳ One way to explore your purpose is to identify what you love, what you're good at, and what the world needs, determining what lies at the intersection of those three things.

PART

THREE

CREATE YOUR JOYFUL EVERYDAY

CHAPTER 7

SETTING JOYFUL GOALS

A NEW APPROACH TO GOAL SETTING

Now that we've spent time exploring what would add more joy to your life, it's time for the most exciting bit: putting everything you've learned into action. It's time to start creating your joyful everyday with some good old-fashioned goal setting.

How does the thought of setting goals make you feel? Does it make you feel excited and ready to dream big, or does it make you feel a little queasy? If it's the latter, you're not alone. For so many of us, goal setting holds negative connotations. Perhaps goals feel like something reserved for the workplace. Maybe you feel a bit reluctant to set yourself new objectives or targets because you've failed to achieve goals you've set in the past. Or maybe you just feel completely overwhelmed and struggle to know where to start.

For so long, I had a terrible relationship with goal setting. I was stuck in a toxic cycle of setting lofty, ambitious goals that reflected the person I thought I *should* be, and then when I inevitably failed to achieve them, I'd use that failure as evidence to back up the negative thoughts I had about myself. Every unachieved goal provided extra fuel for the fire that was my limiting beliefs, extra proof that I was lazy or selfish or unmotivated or stupid. The goals I set were always about giving things up or expecting myself to be perfect. They didn't add joy to my life or help me to prioritise the things that made me happy. In fact, they did quite the opposite. No wonder I always struggled to stick to them.

If that resonates with you, if you too have found yourself in a bit of a toxic relationship with goal setting, I want you to know that there's a different way. It's not the act of setting goals that's the problem—goal setting is simply a tool that we can use. It's how we approach the process that makes the difference. With the right approach, our goals can help us to build a life that feels truly joyful and intentional. In this chapter, we'll discuss that approach. Forget everything you thought you knew about goal setting and get ready to feel excited and energised about the process!

Why Is Goal Setting Even Important?

Let's start by looking at why we need to set goals in the first place. What role do they have in helping us to build a joyful life?

When we approach the process in the right way, our goals can help us to get more intentional about our lives. It can be tempting to believe that living our most joyful lives will happen naturally once we figure out what we want, but we have years of conditioning and societal expectations to unpack that can make it difficult. Our goals can act like a map, providing a sense of direction to help us move from where we currently are to where we want to be. As we'll talk about in later chapters, change can be overwhelming and trigger resistance, but when we have clear goals to work towards, it's easier to implement them.

Research suggests that people with dreams or goals that they're working towards are happier than those who don't have them (Boniwell and Tunariu 2019). There are a few key theories about why this might be. Firstly, goals provide a sense of purpose and a reason for being. In the words of Viktor Frankl, they are the "why of living." Secondly, our goals can provide structure and meaning to our daily lives, helping us to figure out how to manage our time. And finally, making progress towards our goals can boost our confidence and self-esteem.

Nearly all of the research in the field of goal theory suggests that it's the pursuit of and progression made towards our goals that enhance our well-being, as opposed to actually achieving the goal. In other words, when it comes to our goals, it's the journey rather than the outcome that's most important.

What Makes A Joyful Goal?

So, now that we know why goals are important, it's time to think about what makes a good goal. In fact, we're not just shooting for good goals here; we're shooting for goals that feel truly joyful. Goals that feel exciting, energising, and motivating. Those goals will look different for all of us, but there are a few key ingredients that all joyful goals require.

Joyful goals should be . . .

Intrinsically Motivated

Our goals must be motivated by our own personal satisfaction, as opposed to being driven by a need to impress or seek validation from others. Another way to consider the difference is that with intrinsic goals, we find some enjoyment in the pursuit of the goal itself (we do them for the sake of doing them), whereas extrinsic goals are often driven by a desire for something else, such as money (we seek them for the sake of something else).

For example, a goal to take a walk every day because you enjoy it and you know it improves your mental health would be intrinsically motivated; a goal to work out every day because you want to look a certain way on vacation would be extrinsically motivated. One goal is inherently meaningful and focuses on personal satisfaction and enjoyment, whereas the other goal has little inherent enjoyment and uses an external measure of success (appearance).

Approach Focused

Research suggests that the best goals are approach oriented, meaning that you're moving towards something you want instead of moving away from something less desirable. So often, we set goals focused on avoiding something—we save money to avoid falling into debt, we exercise to avoid poor health, we work harder to avoid feeling like a failure around our friends. But psychologists have found that these types of goals add to the stress we feel, and that we're more likely to experience the benefits of goal setting if we focus on approach goals—goals focused on improving something.

Try to get into the habit of making your goals as positive as possible. If we take the examples above, we can see how much more energising and exciting they feel when we look at them through an approach focus: saving money to feel abundant and free, exercising to sleep better and feel healthier, and working hard to feel more confident and fulfilled. These approaches feel a lot more motivating, right?

Authentic

If our goals don't feel authentic to us, then we aren't likely to enjoy pursuing them. One way to ensure that our goals are authentic is to check them against our values. If your goal feels like it's getting you closer to living in alignment with your values, it's probably an authentic goal. If it feels in conflict with your values, it's not going to add more joy to your life.

When setting goals, ask yourself if there's a way to use your values to make the process of achieving the goal feel more authentic, too. For example, if you have a goal to save more money and one of your values is fun, make a list of fun things you can do for free. Or if you have a goal to start your own business and one of your values is connection, try to connect with some fellow business owners for a coffee date.

Meaningful

A joyful goal should feel meaningful. You should be able to see how working towards and achieving your goal will get you closer to the vision you have for your life. Your goals should feel connected and purposeful, and the very act of pursuing them should add some value to your life.

A great way to check that your goals are meaningful is to use a tool called "the five whys." The idea is that you take the goal and repeatedly ask yourself why it is important to you, five times. Each consecutive question relates to your previous answer. Here's an example:

My goal is to start my own business.

↝ **Why is that important?**
Because working for myself will allow me to do work that has an impact.

↝ **Why is that important?**
Because doing work that has an impact feels fulfilling to me.

↝ **Why is that important?**
Because if I am fulfilled, I'll be happier and more present.

↝ **Why is that important?**
Because when I'm present, I can be a better friend and partner.

→ **Why is that important?**
Because I know that the relationships in my life bring me a lot of joy, and I want them to be as strong as possible.

If the goal still feels important and worthy to you after five rounds of interrogation, chances are it's a meaningful goal!

Adaptable

Goals can start to feel distinctly un-joyful, or like they're setting us up to fail, when they're too rigid. We all know that life throws us curveballs and that sometimes achieving our goals can feel out of our hands. Taking a flexible approach that can be adapted if necessary is likely to make the process feel a whole lot better.

To employ flexibility, focus less on a specific outcome and more on a direction of travel. If you set a rigid goal of attending the gym three times a week and then miss a session due to traffic or getting sick, it's easy to slip back into the toxic cycle of self-loathing and to give up on your goal completely. However, if your goal is about engaging in some form of exercise each week to feel a little fitter, you can adapt how you do that based on whatever your circumstances are that week.

Fun

Finally, for a goal to feel truly joyful, it should be fun! When my clients are setting goals, I ask, "What is the most joyful way that you could achieve this?" Our society has taught us that the best way to get things done is the quickest or the most efficient way, but when we buy into that, we cut ourselves off from the joy that can be found while working towards a goal.

We know from the research that it's the pursuit of a goal, rather than achieving it, that makes us happy, so stop trying to rush the process! Instead, slow down and give yourself permission to have as much fun as possible working towards your goal.

ATTITUDE HACK

Replace a "lack" goal with a "gain" goal. So, instead of vowing to give something up, create a goal that adds something to your life. By adding more positive stuff to your life, you'll crowd out the negative stuff without having to rely on willpower alone.

For example, instead of setting a goal to stop watching TV, you might set yourself a goal to read more books. Instead of setting a goal to eat less chocolate, you might set yourself a goal to eat more fruit. Instead of setting a goal to spend less on clothes, you might set yourself a goal to save more money for travel.

The Why > How > What Method

So, now that we know what makes a worthwhile goal, it's time to start setting some of our own. Before we do, I want to introduce you to the method I use with my clients and teach in my group programmes, which I refer to as the why > how > what method. This method was inspired by Simon Sinek's brilliant book *Start with Why*, but where Sinek uses this model to look at how businesses can drive leadership and innovation, I use this approach to set goals that feel joyful to us.

This method ensures that our goals feel connected and aligned to the bigger picture we have for our lives. Instead of just plucking goals from thin air and hoping we feel a bit happier when we achieve them (an approach that rarely yields any success), this method allows us to be intentional about where we're focusing our time and energy.

Let's start by breaking down the three steps.

Why

Your *why* is basically what we've spent most of this book exploring so far. It's your vision of what the most joyful version of your life would look like. You can think of it as your reason for wanting to make a change in the first place.

When we think about our *why*, we're thinking about those long-term changes that will help us to maximise the amount of joy we experience day-to-day. For example, perhaps you know that you want to be more present for your children, or that you want a job that feels more impactful and meaningful for you. Maybe you want to spend less time working and more time being creative, or maybe you're feeling pulled to leave the city and relocate to the seaside.

Also consider how you want your life to feel. You can jot down a few words that best describe how you'd love to feel on a perfect average day in your life, and then consider the changes that will invite those feelings in. As with everything in this book, there's no one-size-fits-all *why*, but hopefully, by completing the exercises in the previous chapters, you'll have started to develop a sense of what yours is.

How

The next stage, *how*, explores how you'll shift from where you currently are to that vision you've outlined for your future. You're probably going to have more than one *how*, and you can think of them as loose areas of intention. I encourage my clients to approach this stage by asking themselves which areas of life they need to focus on in the next three to six months to move them closer to their *why*. It's not about having the whole plan figured out now, but rather it's about identifying what you can do in the short-to-medium-term to gain momentum.

As an example, when I first started thinking about changing my career, I set the following *hows* for myself: connecting with people who could help me on this journey (coaches, mentors, etc.); assessing our finances to see how much income our lifestyle would require of my next career move; exploring retraining opportunities; and reading, listening, watching, and engaging with as many career resources as possible. At this stage, I had no idea what my next career move would look like, but by determining my intentions and areas of focus, I was able to set some goals and start working towards my major shift.

What

The aim of the *what* is to get specific and set proper goals. At this stage, we define the actions we'll take to start moving towards our vision. I recommend establishing at least one or two goals for each *how* or area of intention, all of which should feel achievable over a three-month period. Anything longer than that will feel overwhelming, whereas anything that can be achieved in a shorter period probably won't feel substantial enough to move you forward. Be as specific as possible when determining your *whats*—the more you can define your goals and the actions you'll take, the easier it will be to prioritise them in your day-to-day life. Finally, remember how you want to feel as you work on the goals. The fastest, most efficient way won't always be the best way!

To the right is one example of how this method works in action.

There are a few reasons I encourage my clients to use this method. First, it encourages us to think outside the box, to get creative with goals tailored to our authentic selves. It can also help us to focus on the process rather than the outcome, allowing us to hold our goals more gently and practise self-compassion.

Use the why > how > what method to plan out your vision, intentions, and goals for the next couple of months.

Once you've defined your goals, spend a little time thinking about the actions you'll need to take to achieve them. The more you can break action items down at this stage, the easier it will be to stay on track even when life gets busy.

Top tip: write your goals down! A study conducted by Dr. Gail Matthews found that people who wrote their goals down were forty-two percent more likely to achieve them (Gardner and Albee 2015).

The Experiment Approach

Would you believe me if I told you that my current career and business started as an experiment? Maybe not. Maybe you've bought into the idea that successful career pivots or other big life changes require robust, detailed plans to work. Perhaps that's true for some people, but for me, trying to plan everything out never did anything but squash my enthusiasm.

It's not that I didn't try. My decade-long corporate career taught me that

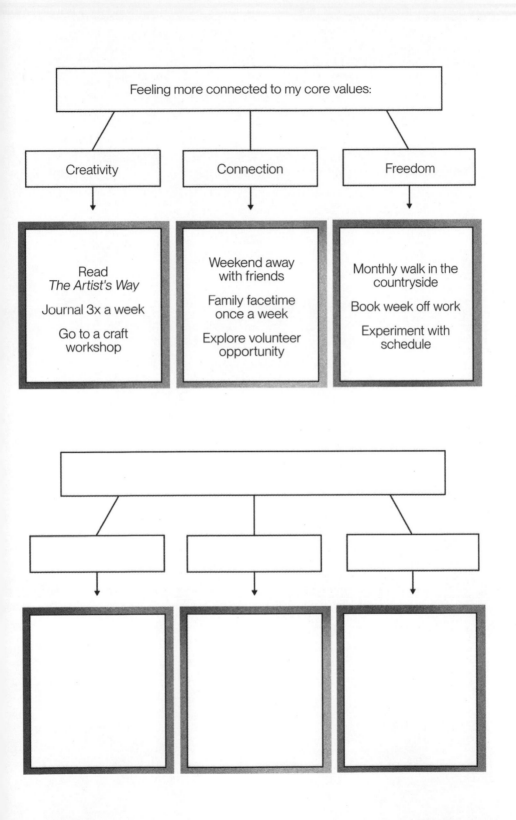

having a strategy was vital to success, so every time I found myself seriously thinking about making a change, I'd go through the following process:

1. Identify the desired change I want to make.
2. Google a plan of how to pivot or seek advice from someone I thought was smarter or more experienced than me.
3. Struggle to implement this plan or advice, as none of it takes into consideration any context of my own life or the resources I have available to me.
4. Fail at making the change, and then use that failure to feed my beliefs that I'm lazy, stupid, weak, or unmotivated.

Perhaps this little routine feels familiar to you. Perhaps you've also been burnt by trying to follow someone else's perfect morning routine or exercise schedule, and then beating yourself up when you couldn't make it work. Perhaps, like me, you've repeated this process over and over, damaging your self-trust in the process. If so, I want to tell you that there is another way to make a change. I call it the experiment approach, the steps of which are as follows:

1. Identify the desired change you want to make.
2. Brainstorm the most joyful ways you could make this change.
3. Plan an experiment around one of your joyful ideas to take some action.
4. Reflect and learn: Was your hypothesis correct? What have you learned for your next experiment?

What I love about this approach is that you can't fail at an experiment; you can only learn something new. Say you have an idea that getting up an hour earlier will create more space for joy in your day. When you try it out for a week, you realise that you're struggling to get up when the alarm goes off and less time in bed is making you grumpier. This realisation doesn't mean your experiment has failed—far from it. You've learned something useful about yourself, and you now have more information to help you plan a better experiment next time. This reframing helps you to stay in a mindset of curiosity and compassion, rather than getting suckered into the idea of perfection.

When I tried this experiment approach, I'd been spending a lot of time trying to figure out what I wanted my next step to be. I'd had plenty of conversations with my coach and mentors, spending months soul-searching, journalling, and reading and listening to just about every career resource available. Through all of that work, I'd started to build confidence in the search for joy. I began to see that helping people find joy might feel like impactful and purposeful work for me.

But I'd been burnt too many times in the past by overzealous commitments and intimidating ambitions, so I made a promise to myself. Instead of piling on the pressure, I'd take a gentler approach. Instead of writing myself long to-do lists or structured strategies, I planned a simple experiment: before I committed to retraining or learning all of the intricacies of how to start a business, I'd start a podcast and see how that went. The podcast was nothing fancy, just me chatting into the cheapest mic I could find on Amazon. But I figured that if I could show up and talk about all things joy and positivity for fifteen to twenty minutes every week, I'd feel confident that this was the path for me. And if not, then I'd have at least picked up some new skills and avoided blowing a load of money on new qualifications I'd never actually use.

For the first time in my life, I approached a new goal in a new way. For the first time, I started a project without having a rigid expectation of what I wanted the outcome to be. The purpose of starting the podcast wasn't to build an audience or to establish myself as some sort of expert (although, over time, it would help me to do both of those things); it was simply to see if I enjoyed it. I wasn't bothered about tracking external measure of success—downloads or chart positions or reviews. I was simply curious about testing my hypothesis. I had an inkling that a new career in the well-being and positive psychology space might feel purposeful and fun, and this new podcast gave me an opportunity to check that my assumption was right. Three and a half years and almost two hundred episodes later, I can safely say that the hypothesis was validated. But even if it hadn't been, I still would have learned something.

When establishing your goals, try to resist the idea that you must set them high. If the most impactful way to make a change was to expect perfection overnight, chances are you'd already have a perfect life and wouldn't be reading this book. Instead, try small, curiosity-fuelled experiments. Be open to what they teach you and build on those lessons. I promise you that the change you're seeking will happen a lot more quickly (and a lot more joyfully!) that way.

LET'S RECAP

✴ When we set them in the right way, goals are the stepping-stones between our current reality and the most joyful vision we have for our lives.

✴ Goal setting is good for our well-being, and research shows that it's the pursuit of the goals that wields the benefits, rather than the achievement of them.

✴ We can set goals that add joy to our lives by ensuring that they're:

   o intrinsically motivated
   o focused on moving towards something better, instead of moving away from something undesirable
   o authentic and aligned with our core values
   o meaningful
   o flexible and adaptable
   o fun

✴ Setting goals that feel like permission slips can act as a reminder to invite in more joy.

✴ The why > how > what method can help you to set goals that feel aligned with your vision. Taking an experimental approach can help you to stay curious and less outcome-focused.

MASTERING YOUR MINDSET

CHAPTER 8

WRITING NEW STORIES FOR YOURSELF

If you have ever tried to make a change in your life, you'll know that setting goals is only the first part of the journey. To bring that change to fruition, you need to keep showing up day after day and taking action. And that's the difficult part, right?

If you struggle to stay on track with your goals, you're not alone. This doesn't indicate that you're doing anything wrong. For the most part, humans don't seek out change. No matter how much your conscious mind is telling you that you're ready to start making changes and prioritising joy, your sub-conscious mind will likely work to throw you off track. Our brains prefer stability, security, and predictability, prioritising these things at all costs—even if that means staying trapped in a life that makes us miserable.

Though our brains may operate differently, there are common mindset blocks or biases that I see coming up time and time again with my clients. In this chapter, I'm going to dive into what some of those blocks and biases are, share some tips on how to counteract them, and give you some tools that you can use to proactively make the process of change feel good.

My hope is that this chapter will help you to see that these mental blocks are normal, but that we must not let them call the shots. By learning about how resistance rears its head, we can prepare ourselves to counteract it and feel more empowered to take action. Plus, you'll hopefully feel a lot less alone hearing that this stuff is something we all struggle with.

Let's jump in.

Things That Get In The Way Of Change

Impostor Syndrome

In 2016, Adele headlined Glastonbury Festival, the biggest music festival in the UK. Glastonbury is one of my favourite events, and Adele is an artist that I love and respect. But as tickets to the festival are rarer than gold dust, I found myself watching her performance on the TV while curled up on my sofa, instead of bellowing along with the crowd as they swayed in a muddy field.

In between performing her hit songs, Adele talked to the audience, sharing anecdotes of her new life in Los Angeles and how pleased she was to be back home for a little while. Adele's onstage chatter is often funny and entertaining, but one anecdote caught my attention above the rest. Just before performing her Oscar- and Grammy-award-winning hit, "Skyfall," which was the title track of the 2012 Bond film, Adele admitted that the first time she was asked to record the James Bond theme, she declined, because she'd thought it was a hoax. Yep, multi-award-winning, chart-topping, platinum-selling artist Adele thought that the request for her to write and sing a soundtrack was a joke.

It was then that I realised that even though I can't hold a single note, and there isn't even a degree of possibility that I'll grace the famous Pyramid Stage during my lifetime, I had something in common with Adele: impostor syndrome. And I'm going to guess that you're in our gang, too, seeing as just about every human I've ever met has suffered from this phenomenon.

Impostor syndrome is defined as "the persistent inability to believe that one's success is deserved or has been legitimately achieved as a result of one's own efforts or skills." It's characterised by that horrible swirling in your stomach as you start to doubt your abilities, or that chilling coldness that descends over you when you start to fear that you're nothing more than a fraud. And never is impostor syndrome more present than when we're trying to make a change.

But your impostor syndrome isn't giving you any valuable information. It isn't a sign that you're on the wrong track. You're not experiencing it because you aren't ready or because you're unqualified. It's just a trick your brain plays on you to try to encourage you to stay within your safe, steady, predictable comfort zone. Trust me: if impostor syndrome truly was a sign that you didn't have enough experience, Adele wouldn't be feeling it, and neither would Michelle Obama, Ryan Reynolds, or Tina Fey, who have all gone on the record to say that they experience it.

Try to start seeing impostor syndrome not as a sign that you're unqualified or about to fall flat on your face, but as a sign that you're showing up to make a change. Put simply, if impostor syndrome is present, it usually means you're about to do something pretty cool.

How to counteract it → Whenever I hear that someone is struggling with impostor syndrome (all of us from time to time), my advice is always the same: start an achievement log. An achievement log is a record of all the things, big and small, that you're achieving. I recommend that people store their achievement logs in a Google Doc, or in the notes section of their phones (that way you always have access to it), and to set up a regular reminder to update it (I like to do mine every Friday afternoon). Then, whenever your reminder pings, spend ten to fifteen minutes writing down all the things you've achieved that week. It's important to include both the big and small things and to not worry if your lists start to become repetitive. The point isn't to have the most exciting, unique achievement logs; it's simply to keep a record of the action you're taking and the things you're achieving. Over time, you'll start to build up a strong bank of evidence of your successes to counteract any of the mean things your impostor syndrome might be telling you.

Fear of Failure

Often fuelled by impostor syndrome is another mental block—fear of failure. In a society that tells us that success is our social capital, it's little wonder that we're all so scared of failing. But when that fear of failure stops us from showing up for our dreams, we're already failing ourselves.

A fear of failure can show up in many ways. Sometimes it manifests as perfection, keeping us so stuck in the planning process that we never actually reach the stage of taking action. It can cause us to play small, setting goals and targets that feel easy and attainable so that we don't risk missing the mark. Fear of failure can also lead to a sense of indecisiveness or avoidance, causing us to worry so much about making the wrong choice that we never actually choose anything.

And that's the real problem with a fear of failure: it makes us believe that there's a right way of doing something. It tries to convince us that there's only one perfect path, and that if we choose anything other than that, we'll appear stupid or naive. And it teaches us that failure is something to avoid at all costs, denying us access to the rich learnings and growth moments that come from giving something a go, regardless of the outcome.

I believe that one of the most powerful tools we have in overcoming a fear of failure is to get clear on what we're scared of. Fear of failure is a broad term that doesn't reveal any information about what we're actually worried about. Cleverly, our brains evade the specificity of the problem because if we know with specific detail what is troubling us, we can start to formulate a plan to mitigate those worries, even overcome them. But if the fear feels vague and overwhelming, clouding the truth of what we fear, we tend to remain paralysed by it.

I was afraid to fail when I had to choose between accepting a promotion or leaving my job to pursue self-employed life. As I described earlier, my gut instinct told me that the latter option was the best fit for me and checking in with my values helped to validate that, but that didn't mean the fear of failure was any less overwhelming. I remember crying on the phone to my mum, telling her that I was too scared to take the risk. What if it all went wrong? Because my mum is wise and forever calm in a crisis, instead of indulging in my hysteria, she simply asked me this: "What exactly are you scared of?"

That question was powerful because it shifted me out of catastrophising and into planning mode. To start, I worried what my colleagues might think. That felt less scary to me once I articulated it. I worried about making ends meet, feeling unsure about how to find clients. That still terrified me, but by identifying those worries, I was able to figure out what I needed to do to make the prospect of leaving my job feel less scary.

Facing our fears can feel like a scary process, but it's a vital one if we want to make a change. And I promise you, once you look your fear of failure in the eye, it won't have nearly as much power over you anymore.

How to counteract it → Picture your worst-case scenario. This might seem counterintuitive—surely if you're scared of failure, picturing that failure in full colour will only enhance that fear, right? Well, usually, that isn't the case. We tend to realise that if we get the courage to pursue our goals and things don't go to plan, we'll simply end up back where we are right now. You can then picture your best-case scenario—where you'll end up if everything goes to plan. Now, instead of feeling that pursuing goals involves some huge risk, you may realise that the two outcomes are staying where you are or achieving everything you dream of. Not so scary after all, eh?

Fear of Success

There seems to be a lot written about the fear of failure, but something I don't see discussed as often is the fear of success. And yet, hundreds of hours coaching my clients through big changes has shown me that often, it's a fear of success that's truly holding them back. But don't we all want to achieve the goals we set for ourselves? Surely, we all want to appear successful in the eyes of our peers and loved ones? That might be the case in our conscious minds, but subconsciously, there's more at play.

To understand why we might fear success, we need to understand humanity's desire to fit in and belong. As we discussed in Chapter Two, our psyches are hardwired to want to belong to part of a pack. We all have an urge to feel part of a collective, and sometimes that urge can impact how we show up.

So, what does any of this have to do with success? If deep down you worry that achieving all of your goals will risk your role in your pack or community, your subconscious will do everything it can to prevent that success. And while we might have been sold the narrative that it's the most successful people who are the most popular, reality often differs. Maybe you grew up in a town where people with big dreams were gossiped about (the "Who does she think she is?" mentality) and you're worried about being the victim of everyone's bitching sessions. Maybe you worry that if you move to a new location, you'll be forgotten about by your group of friends. Maybe you fear that if you find a job you actually enjoy, you'll lose touch with the working-class identity that shaped your formative years.

Whatever your worry, if there's even the slightest inkling that making the change will cost you socially, you're likely to encounter some resistance.

How to counteract it → Often our fear of success plays out on a subconscious level, but bringing conscious thought to it can help to quash any worries. Spend some time thinking about the people who are rooting for you and consider how achieving your goals will positively impact the people you love and care about. More joy for you usually means more joy for the people around you, too.

Sunk-Cost Fallacy

Have you ever stayed in a relationship that wasn't serving you just because you'd been in it for so long? Have you ever kept investing in a project that wasn't right just because you'd already spent some money on that project? Have you ever stayed in a job you hated just because you had to train for a long time to get it? If you answered yes to any of those questions, you've experienced sunk-cost fallacy.

A phrase originally coined by the business world, sunk-cost fallacy describes our biases towards decisions or behaviours that support things we've already invested time, money, or emotional energy into. Put simply, if we've already spent something on an idea or endeavour, we're more likely to follow through with it, even if we know that the idea or endeavour isn't working out in our best interests.

Sunk-cost fallacy can be prevalent when it comes to making a change in our lives, often getting in the way of us taking action. One of the things that held me back from getting started with my career change was the thought of all of the blood, sweat, and tears I'd put into building the level of credibility and respect I'd amassed in my previous career. I'd spent ten years climbing up the corporate ladder, sacrificing quality time with loved ones, sleep, and sometimes even my own health to secure those much-lusted after promotions and accolades.

Therefore, even though I knew that my career was making me miserable, I found it difficult to contemplate making a change. I spent every waking hour complaining about my job, and I'd chat to anyone who'd listen about all of the reasons why I knew I wasn't on the right career path, but whenever I thought about leaving, all I could focus on was the community, experience, and validation I'd be letting go of if I did.

Sunk-cost fallacy is a cognitive bias, something our brains do automatically with little input from our conscious mind. But being aware of it is the first step in overcoming it. The key is to focus on the word *fallacy*—our brains might lead us to believe that the things we've already invested in are more worthy, but often that isn't true. There might be a better, more joyful option waiting for us, but we're too busy getting in our own way to see it.

It's important to remember that you have a choice. You have the power to make a change for the better, you can pivot or start over no matter how much you've already invested. When you do, magic can happen.

How to counteract it → If you're finding it difficult to make a change because of the time, money, or energy you've already invested into a previous decision, try zooming out. You might feel like walking away from your current reality is a waste, but how will you feel in ten years' time if you don't make a change? What will you be sacrificing by continuing along the same path? Instead of letting the potential for current regret keep you stuck, harness the power of future regret to help you make a change.

✦ A Sprinkle OF JOY ✦

Write a "done" list at the end of each day. So many of us leave the office every evening focusing on all the things we didn't manage to tick off our to-do lists, but how many of us give ourselves a pat on the back for all of the things we *did* manage to do? I'm guessing not many of us, but I'm on a mission to change that!

A done list is a list of all the things you've done that day. It will take you less than a minute or two to write, but the impact of that little list is powerful. It'll help free you from your negativity bias and focus on the things you accomplished.

Limiting Beliefs

Limiting beliefs are exactly as they sound—beliefs that place limitations on us in some way. They're perhaps the most dangerous mental blocks that we've discussed in this chapter because, most of the time, we've been carrying them around with us for so long that we don't recognise them as beliefs, instead seeing them as objective truths or facts.

To illustrate this point, I want to share a story about how a limiting belief held me back from joy. I was a nerdy kid, performing well in all of my classes with one exception: PE I wasn't blessed with coordination or speed, so team sports were never my thing, and given that the PE curriculum in the UK is pretty much made up of netball, hockey, and cross-country running, I struggled to keep up and often felt like I was falling behind my classmates.

This might not have been such a problem if I'd had a teacher who was encouraging and compassionate, but unfortunately, I had quite the opposite. Before long, I'd internalised her criticisms and my own shame at struggling to keep up. I started to believe that I was terrible at exercise. In time, that belief crystallised into a fact in my mind, becoming the bedrock of my identity, where it would stay until my early twenties. When my peers at university asked if I was going to join a sports club, I'd say, "Nope, I don't do exercise." When my friends invited me along to a new yoga class, I'd say, "Thanks but no thanks. I don't do exercise." And when my now husband and I first started dating and he invited me to join him for a hike in the countryside, I couldn't have shot him down more quickly: "Sorry, I don't do exercise. How about we go to the cinema instead?"

It was only when I attended a course for work when I was twenty-three and learned about limiting beliefs that I realised I wasn't physically incapable of exercise—I'd just developed a belief that I was. It was a huge mic-drop moment for me, and that year I went on to run two marathons. I was painfully slow (an incredible woman running her first marathon in her seventies beat me) and I haven't kept the running habit up, but it felt so powerful to reclaim my narrative and tear up that limiting belief once and for all. Since then, I've found so much joy in dancing, swimming, cycling, hiking, and lifting weights that I never would have found if I'd kept on carrying that limiting belief.

I've seen the same transformation happen for my clients, one of whom believed she was too shy to present in front of an audience because her parents and classmates were always commenting on how quiet and reserved she was. These days, public speaking is a big part of her job, and she gets a real thrill from standing on stage and sharing her story. Another client believed she wasn't creative because at school she was only ever praised for her academic success. These days, she runs an incredibly successful graphic design business. Yet another client thought she wasn't very clever because she didn't leave school with any qualifications. Now she spends her time consulting for huge organisations, delivering incredible game-changing work and serving as a thought leader in her industry.

What I hope you take from this is a reminder that just because you've held a limiting belief for a long period of time, that doesn't mean it's a fact. You have the power to let go of the belief or to replace it with something more useful.

How to counteract it → Whenever my clients are feeling held back by a negative thought or belief, I ask them three questions:

1. **Is this a belief or a fact?**

   First, we must establish whether the thought you have is a fact or a belief. If you believe your thought to be a fact, what evidence do you have to back it up? Is it a permanent truth, or could it change in the future? At this stage, it's rare that something is an absolute fact. Rather, it's a belief that we might have been carrying around for a long time.

2. **If it's a belief, what else could I choose to believe?**

   Once we've established that the thought you have is a belief and not a fact, we can then acknowledge that it's something we're choosing to believe in. And when we do that, it helps us to see that we can choose to believe something new. At this stage, choose a new belief that will serve you better, a belief that will help you in your pursuit to live a more joyful life.

3. **What evidence can I find to support this new belief?**

   Finally, once you've chosen this new belief, try to find some evidence to back the new belief up. This will help you to adopt and trust in the new belief more seamlessly. You could look for evidence from your own life (e.g., Have you demonstrated the quality you want to have before?). Or you could find people who have travelled a similar journey as you, who can provide hope that it's possible.

To show you this example in action, let's revisit the negative thought I had about not being able to exercise.

1. **Is this a belief or a fact?**

   Well, as no doctor ever told me I was physically incapable of exercise, I could see that it was a belief—albeit one I'd been carrying around for a long time.

2. **If it's a belief, what else could I choose to believe?**

   I could choose to believe that, regardless of my skill level or ability, I could find joy in movement. I could choose to believe that exercise takes many forms outside of team sports. I could choose to believe that perhaps I hadn't found the right form of exercise for me yet.

3. **What evidence can I find to support this new belief?**

    I enjoyed dancing as a child; perhaps I could find joy in it again. I've seen friends take up hiking in the countryside, which looks quite fun. I used to love swimming but haven't been for a little while—why not go again?

It can be tempting to believe that with the right tools or actions, we can eliminate these mindset blocks from our lives. In my own experience, and what I've witnessed with clients, it's rare that we eliminate them completely, as many are hardwired into our psyches. But we can minimise the impact they have on us.

So, try not to beat yourself up if a limiting belief rears its ugly head or you experience a bout of impostor syndrome. Use this method, alongside the other tools I've shared in this book, to challenge those limiting beliefs, take back the power of choice, and look at your beliefs from different, often more joyful, perspectives.

One of the best tools to boost our confidence and master our mindset is to visualise success. This tool has long been used in sports psychology and coaching. Studies show that it works because the neurons in our brain interpret imagery as equivalent to a real-life action. Therefore, when we visualise something, our brain creates a new neural pathway that primes our body to act in a way consistent to what we imagined. Pretty cool, huh? It can also help us to become familiar with our own version of success, making it feel less scary or overwhelming, which in turn makes us less likely to slip into self-sabotage mode.

Visualising success is also incredibly simple to do—just think about what the most joyful version of your life would look like and spend a little time in your daydream. Try to be specific: imagine a day from start to end, picturing everything from what you'd have for your breakfast, to the clothes you'd wear, to the way you'd feel as you climbed into bed.

Do this as often as you can, and over time, you'll start to find that you feel more motivated, more primed for action, and more optimistic about the future.

YOU HAVE THE POWER TO LET GO OF LIMITING BELIEFS

LET'S RECAP

✳ Making a change isn't as simple as setting goals and taking action because our brains resist change. We like to stay in our safe, steady, predictable comfort zones.

✳ This resistance to change can present itself in many ways, including:

- o Impostor syndrome
- o Fear of failure
- o Fear of success
- o Sunk-cost-fallacy thinking
- o Limiting beliefs

✳ Experiencing these mindset blocks is completely normal, but there are things we can do to minimise their impact, from acknowledging our fears to visualising success, focusing on our achievements, and challenging our limiting beliefs.

STAYING

THE

CHAPTER 9

COURSE

MAKING YOUR JOYFULLY EVER AFTER STICK

When we first started mapping out the vision for this book, I told my wonderful editor that I wanted it to be three things: practical, meaningful, and impactful. As you've probably gathered over the course of this book, I'm not interested in surface-level change. The work that truly excites me is helping my clients to make the changes that have a meaningful and lasting impact on their lives. With that in mind, there was only one note I could end this book on: staying the course.

I wish that making a change was as simple as gaining new knowledge and putting it into action, but we all know that it isn't quite as straightforward as that. And that's not because we're doing anything wrong—it's because we're human. Our levels of motivation and determination ebb and flow like tides. Confidence takes time to develop and grow. Life has a habit of throwing curveballs when we least expect them. Sometimes, no matter how focused or prepared we are, things go off track.

We must be open about that because if we're not—if we try to turn a blind eye to the realities of life and power on naively—we only set ourselves up for more misery and stress, the very things we're trying to avoid. Instead, we must accept the fact that sometimes even the best laid plans go awry. Let's let that thought empower us rather than scare us. When we accept the realities of life, we set ourselves up for greater success.

If you have ever listened to a guided meditation before, you will have heard the idea that meditation isn't about completely clearing the mind—it's about noticing that you've been distracted (which inevitably happens to all of us, because clearing our minds is an impossible expectation!), and then returning to whatever it is that you're focusing on, whether that be your breath, a mantra, or a sensation within your body. This serves as an analogy for choosing joy. Just as it's impossible to completely clear our minds, it's impossible to completely clear our life of obstacles. You will go on vacation and lose touch with the habits you've been building. Work will get extra busy, and you'll find yourself with less time on your hands. Your focus will get pulled in a different direction as your friends and family require extra support. All of these things are completely normal. It's how you respond to these bumps in the road that matters.

Instead of letting them derail us, instead of using them as evidence that we're bad people or that we'll never make a change, we can practise that same method used in meditation: notice the bumps in the road, then refocus. Acknowledge that things have gone off track, then get back to choosing joy. That's the only way to make the changes you're seeking—imperfectly, messily, humanly.

In this final chapter, we'll explore tools and ideas to help you in the process of noticing and refocusing. I'll also share some thoughts on how to keep choosing joy when life gets tough and remind you of the importance of focusing on what you can control. Let's jump in.

The Power Of Reflection

If a key part of staying the course and making lasting, impactful change is noticing when we've gone off track, we must improve our powers of perception. In an ideal world, we'd have so much free time for pondering and pottering that this would come naturally to us, but most of us are so busy running from one thing to another that we barely have time to consider what we're going to have for dinner.

Therefore, we need a tool to help us: reflection. Reflection can take many forms, but essentially, it means carving out some time to check in with yourself and how you're feeling. I like to think of these check-ins as little dates with my intuition, an opportunity to get to know myself better and to remind myself of what I want from life. It also allows me to notice when my focus might have shifted in another direction.

How often you build reflection into your life is up to you. You could sit down and journal at the start of every day, or maybe you just want to take a pause once a month to see how everything is feeling. What's important is to make that regular date with yourself. That way, you're never going too long without reminding yourself of what's most important to you and considering what needs to change to help you prioritise those things. Again, how you choose to reflect is up to you, but I'd like to offer up the questions I use during my reflective check-ins as a guide:

→ What has felt good about my life today/this week/this month?

→ What has felt challenging today/this week/this month?

→ What have I learned today/this week/this month?

→ What progress have I made towards my goals today/this week/this month?

→ Is there anything I'd like to change as a result of these reflections?

It sounds simple, but getting into the habit of asking yourself these five questions (or similar questions that provoke your thinking) on a regular basis will make the process of noticing and refocusing so much easier.

Reflection isn't just important for noticing when we've gone off track; it can also help us be aware of when some of the experiments or goals we've planned haven't delivered the outcome we'd been hoping for.

Back in those early days of self-employment, when I was still navigating what my business would look like and which services I wanted to offer, something that felt exciting to me was to host some in-person events. I loved the idea of being in a room with people talking about all things joy, and the idea aligned with my values of connection, creativity, and making an impact. So, I got straight into planning mode, researching venues, and mapping out a whole roster of events for the year ahead.

In January 2020, I hosted the first couple, and on paper, they were a roaring success—both events sold out, and the feedback from participants was great. But when I sat down for my usual check-in that week, I noticed that things didn't feel quite right. Sure, I'd loved being in-person with people and guiding them through tools and techniques that could help them invite more joy into their lives, but there was a lot of stuff that came with running an event that I didn't love, like all of the admin involved—ordering lunch, checking building regulations, buying the right type of insurance. I didn't love the pressure of trying to sell all of the tickets before the deadline. I didn't love the stress I felt on the day as I tried to make sure everything ran smoothly. Upon reflecting, I could see that the joy I felt delivering the workshop was outweighed by a whole load of overwhelm, and that if I continued with the events I had planned for the rest of the year, I'd burn out pretty damn quickly.

This anecdote is an example of how twenty minutes spent checking in saved me a whole load of misery and stress further down the line. By taking the time to notice how I was feeling, instead of letting the more traditional markers of success guide me, I was able to pivot and focus my energy on the parts of my business that I really loved, such as one-on-one coaching or creating content. This not only helped me to prioritise joy, but it also helped me to have a greater impact with my work, as I felt more excited and inspired.

In the words of John Dewey, philosopher, psychologist, and educational reformer, "We do not learn from experience . . . we learn from reflecting on experience." You might feel that you're too busy to check in, but it will save you time and energy in the long run.

✦ A Sprinkle OF JOY ✦

Get into the habit of starting your morning by asking yourself how you'd like to feel that day. Then, once you've identified the feeling you want to invite in, jot down two to three things you could do that day to bring that feeling to fruition.

This is a simple task that won't take you more than five minutes, but it ties together reflection, intention, and action in a way that helps to create a big impact!

The Importance Of Celebration

Now that we've talked about the power of reflection, let's turn our attention to something else that can help us stay the course: celebrating our wins. Now, this isn't something that has ever come very naturally to me—in fact, I used to avoid it like the plague. I was an expert at shrugging off compliments, downplaying my wins, and moving straight onto the next goal without pausing for breath. But after reading about how important self-celebration is for building confidence and experiencing joy, I've made a concerted effort to get better at it. I believe that taking the time to reflect and feel proud of my progress has helped me to make the changes in my life that have brought me so much joy.

When it comes to celebrating our wins, most of us have some room for improvement. And it's important that we do improve, because celebrating our achievements has a whole host of benefits. Firstly, celebrating our wins, both big and small, helps to build our sense of confidence and self-efficacy. By taking some time to reflect on what we've achieved, we internalise our successes and feel more capable of taking on the next challenge or goal on our journey. Secondly, recognising our achievements creates positive emotions. In Chapter One, we discussed the broaden-and-build theory, which demonstrates that experiencing positive emotions helps to boost our creativity and resilience. But perhaps most importantly, celebrating our wins allows us to be present and savour the things we've worked hard to build in our lives. There's a phrase I love and think about often: *Remember when you wanted what you currently have.* Reflecting on and feeling proud of our achievements helps us to do exactly this—revel in the things we now have that we used to spend time dreaming about, instead of simply ticking a box and moving on to a new dream.

It's up to you how you choose to celebrate your wins, but I recommend setting some mini milestones that can act as prompts to pause and reflect. All of the research in this area suggests that celebrating the incremental steps is more powerful than waiting until you've fully completed your goal, so think about the points on your journey that will act as your mini markers of success. It's important to choose these markers in advance, because as you take action and your confidence grows, you'll forget just how meaningful some of those steps on your journey have been. And remember, these markers of success are yours to define. You don't only get to celebrate the stuff that looks shiny or worthy to others. Give yourself permission to embrace every milestone that feels meaningful to you.

If you need some ideas on how to celebrate those wins of yours, let me offer up a few suggestions . . .

→ Write about how it feels to make the progress you're making. Reflect on the action you've been taking and allow yourself to feel proud.

→ Treat yourself! Even something small like grabbing a coffee or cooking your favourite meal will help you to feel like you've marked the occasion.

→ Consider sharing your wins with others. Research shows that the more you share your successes with loved ones (and the more you cheer them on when they share theirs), the more satisfied you will feel in your relationships.

→   Savour what you've achieved. If you've followed the process in this book, achieving your goals means you've moved closer to the most joyful version of your life. Revel in the joy you've created for yourself!

→   Say a little "thank you" to yourself. Showing yourself some gratitude and feeling thankful for the choices you've made is a brilliant way to celebrate.

Set up a regular reflective practice that works for you. Consider how regularly you'd like to check in and perhaps outline the questions you'd like to use, and then set a date. As we've discussed, when life gets busy, it's easy to forget to reflect, so pop something in your diary to remind yourself.

Give yourself permission to make your reflection check-ins as joyful as possible. You don't want them to become just another thing to add to your to-do list. Instead, create a little ritual out of them—maybe take yourself to your favourite coffee shop, use a specific notebook, or light some candles to make your space feel cosy before you begin. The more inviting you make your reflection dates, the more likely you'll be to make time for them.

Finding Joy During Periods Of Challenge Or Uncertainty

This book has been an exploration of joy—of what it means to us, of the benefits prioritising it can bring us, of ways we can invite more of it into our lives. But what do we do when things get complicated? What do we do when the unexpected strikes and we find ourselves in a period of challenge or uncertainty? What role does joy have in our lives when we're grieving or heartbroken or our jobs are at risk? Where does joy fit in when we're battling illness or poor mental health, when we feel lonely, when we're unsure of what the next stage of life will hold?

It would be easy to make the case that there is no room for joy at times like these. That to try to find joy when we are grieving or lonely or depressed is nothing but an act of toxic positivity. But I'd like to offer up a different perspective: when life feels hard, joy is more important than ever. Because, as we've discussed many times in this book, joy fortifies us. It gives us strength. It gives us a reason to keep on going, even when times get hard.

I'm not encouraging you to ignore those other feelings, to push down negative emotions and to simply focus on joy. Instead, I want to remind you that joy can coexist amongst the sadness and the worry and fear and uncertainty. Joy can not only live alongside those things, but it can make them a little easier to deal with. During the most difficult periods of my own life, it was focusing on those little slivers of joy that kept me getting out of bed, day after day. It was feeling grateful for the good parts of life that gave me the strength to deal with the heartbreaking bits. It was prioritising a little moment of joy each day that allowed me to support my loved ones and bear witness to their pain.

Joy didn't always make me feel less lonely or grief-stricken or angry or sad, but it did help me to keep navigating my way through those emotions. And it gave me hope that something better lay on the other side of the heartache I was experiencing. That hope felt like a life raft at times.

So, if you find yourself in a place where life feels hard, don't give up on joy. It might take a different form, and it might not feel as easy to access, but it's there. And tuning into it will help you get through whatever it is you're going through—I promise you.

Here are some of my best tips for finding joy during periods of challenge and uncertainty:

→ Focus on the little things. Big joys might feel inaccessible to you when life feels hard, so instead, try to turn your attention to the small things. A hot cup of tea, a little glimmer of sunshine, your favourite song playing on the radio. Focusing on these little things can provide just the boost you need.

→ Come back to the present moment. We can spend a lot of time ruminating when we feel stressed or sad, so try coming back to the present and being in your body for a little while. If you find that challenging, try engaging your five senses—what can you see, hear, smell, taste, and feel?

→ Let go of the guilt. I know from experience that trying to find glimmers of joy during a challenging time can make us feel guilty, particularly if we're grieving or supporting someone else, but try to let go of that guilt. Guilt is a mostly useless emotion—it doesn't make things better for anybody else; it only makes you feel worse. Remember that those little moments of joy will increase your capacity to navigate this time.

→ Get outside. When times are hard, it can be useful to get some perspective, and I find the best way to do that is to get outside. There's something about looking up at the constellations above us or watching nature roll on regardless of our own troubles that reminds us that this moment right now is just a tiny blip in the life of the cosmos.

→ Give yourself some grace. Now is the time for a heavy dose of self-compassion. Don't expect yourself to be perfect or put pressure on yourself to feel a certain way. Instead, tune into whatever you're craving right now and try to honour those needs.

→ Trust that this too shall pass. If joy truly feels too difficult to access at this moment, just know that you will experience it again one day. You will laugh and dance and sing and feel hopeful once more.

ATTITUDE HACK

Focus on what you can control. This little mantra is something I held onto during the pandemic lockdowns. Instead of worrying about the cancelled work events and vacations or stressing about when I might get to see my family again, I focused on the things that were within my control. What that looked like was turning every mealtime into an event—laying the table, lighting a candle, working my way through the recipes that I'd been dying to try. It looked like sending my loved ones handwritten mail, so that I still felt connected to them. It looked like showing up for my clients and supporting them in every way I could.

Focusing on what I could control didn't change the circumstances. But it did give me something positive to focus on and helped me to find a little joy in every day, no matter how tricky things got.

FOCUS

ON WHAT

YOU CAN

CONTROL

LET'S RECAP

✳ It's important to accept that life will throw us curveballs, and sometimes we'll go off track. This doesn't mean we've failed; it simply means we're human.

✳ If we find that we've gone off track, we simply need to notice and then get back to choosing joy. Checking in regularly to reflect can help us to do this.

✳ Celebrating our wins is an important part of staying the course. It helps us to internalise our successes, build our confidence and self-esteem, and enjoy the changes we make to our lives.

✳ While it might feel hard to find joy during difficult times, that's when we need it most. Try to focus on any sliver of joy you can find and allow it to strengthen and fortify you.

✳ Focusing on what we can control helps us to find joy even when things feel worrying or uncertain.

FOUR

ONE HUNDRED DAYS OF JOYFUL HABITS

ONE HUNDRED DAYS OF JOYFUL HABITS

Throughout the course of this book, we've been on a journey. We've looked at why we're all experiencing a collective malaise and how joy can help us bounce back from burnout. We've explored where we often go wrong when we try to make joyful changes. We've reviewed what science has to say about inviting more positivity into our lives. We've played around with the tools that can help us find our most authentic definition of joy, and we've thought about how we start to build a life that feels as joyful on the inside as it looks on the outside. Now it's time to put everything we've learnt into action.

One of the best ways to ensure changes last is to make joy a habit—doing something joyful each day instead of saving it all up for holidays or week-ends. With that in mind, I've put together a list of activities to get you started. I've shared ninety ideas of little things you could do to prioritise joy, and I've left space for you to add ten ideas (or more!) of your own, using what you've learned about yourself and what brings you joy throughout the course of this book. Aim to get into the habit of doing at least one thing each day that brings you joy. If a joyful moment doesn't come naturally to you one day, you can skim this list and find an idea that fits with how you're feeling or what time you have available.

These prompts have been organised into the foundations of joy we discussed in Chapters Four and Five. I've also added a section for some bonus prompts to help you find an extra little bit of magic! Instead of approaching these activities or prompts like a to-do list, try to view them as one hundred little permission slips. Because that's what they are: permission slips to invite more joy, ease, and fun into your everyday life, and permission to reap the benefits along the way.

Enjoy!

Connection

→ Print some photos of happy memories with your favourite people and display them in your home.

→ Speak to a friend or loved one on the phone, noticing how it feels to hear their voice.

→ Make a list of the people you feel most connected to in your life. How can you show them a little more love?

→ Write a card for a loved one and pop it in the post. There's something very special about handwritten notes in our digital age, and the act of picking out a card and writing a message will help you to feel connected.

→ Make a list of ways you could get involved with your community. Is there a certain action you feel most drawn to?

→ Strike up a conversation with a stranger in your neighbourhood. A quick chat with your barista or a polite exchange with the courier can go a long way in helping you to feel connected.

→ Share a funny meme or a happy memory with a friend you haven't seen for a while.

→ Practise active listening. Ask someone a question and focus on their answer.

→ People watch. Find a comfy spot somewhere there are lots of people around (such as a café or park). Listen and watch as the world goes on around you. What do you notice?

Experiences Over Things

→ Reclaim your lunch hour and use it to do something fun.

→ Do something that would make your inner child happy: engage in arts and crafts, make daisy chains, play football, watch a nostalgic movie, or dance it out to the songs you loved when you were little. Reconnect with that inner child and notice how joyful it feels to embrace that sense of playfulness.

→ Plan something fun for the month ahead.

→ Make a list of ten fun things (big and small!) that you'd love to do in the season ahead.

→ Make a list of places you'd love to visit in your lifetime.

→ Make something with your hands—bake, sew, paint, garden. It doesn't matter what you choose, only that you notice how it feels to reconnect to the physical.

→ Take some time to reminisce about one of the most fun experiences you've ever had.

→ Visit somewhere in your town or city that you've never been to before. A trip to a new café, exhibition, or park can make you feel like you've had a mini adventure.

Savouring

→ Use something you usually save for special occasions. Spritz your favourite perfume, write in that beautiful notebook, or light the fancy candle!

→ Take an "awe walk," a walk around your local surroundings, but with an attitude of wonder.

→ Try to see your local area through the eyes of a tourist. What's special about it? What looks extra beautiful today? What can you feel inspired by?

→ Make one of your meals feel like an occasion. Lay the table, play your favourite music, and savour the act of dining.

→ Watch a sunrise or sunset.

→ Step outside after the sun has set and look up at the sky. What can you see? How does it feel to give the moon and stars some attention?

→ Choose one mundane or routine element of your day that you want to savour. For example, your first cup of coffee of the day or driving your kids to school. How does savouring the moment change your experience of it?

→ Take a photo of something that brings you joy and share it, whether texting it to a friend or posting on social media.

→ Try to savour your shower. Notice how the water feels as it washes over you, paying attention to the smell and feel of the products you use, and give yourself a head massage as you wash your hair.

→ Stand at your window for five minutes. What can you see happening outside? Can you spot anything you've never noticed before?

Moving

→ Make a playlist of all your favourite feel-good songs, and then play it loud while you dance it out.

→ Get out for a walk in the fresh air, noticing how it makes you feel. Try to engage all of your senses—what can you see, hear, smell, taste, and feel?

→ Make a list of all the ways you used to love to move your body as a child. Can you re-embrace any of them now?

→ Try a form of exercise you've always wanted to try. Let go of the worry of being a beginner and focus on the joy it will bring you.

→ Spend five to ten minutes stretching your body.

→ Practise some yoga. You can find some great free classes and sequences on YouTube.

→ Challenge yourself to spend less time sitting down.

→ Go for a walk in a blue or green space.

→ Practise box breathing. Breathe in slowly to the count of four, hold your breath for four seconds, exhale slowly to the count of four, and then pause for four more seconds. Repeat until you feel re-centred.

→ Practise the basics today—eat well, move your body, and try to get to bed on time.

Practising Kindness

→ Make a list of ten things about yourself that deserve celebrating.

→ Give two compliments: one to yourself and one to someone else.

→ Write a positive review for a service you've received recently.

→ Reach out to someone who might be having a difficult time and offer your support.

→ Make a list of ways you can be kinder to the planet.

→ Find a way to support a cause you care about. Remember, if donating money isn't an option for you, volunteering your time or skills can be even more valuable.

→ Find a way to "pay it forward." Here are some ideas: pay for an extra coffee, tick something off someone else's to-do list, or share a piece of useful advice.

→ Write a list of all the things you've achieved in the past week. How will you celebrate your wins?

→ Tell one of your friends or loved ones what you love most about them.

Lifelong Learning

→ Make a list of things you're curious about in life.

→ Listen to a podcast or watch a video about something you've always been interested in.

→ Carve out half an hour to read.

→ Try out a new recipe.

→ Make a list of skills you'd love to master. Do you know anyone who might be able to help you?

→ Spend fifteen minutes practising something you'd like to be better at.

→ Make a list of the best advice you've received or lessons that you've learned from other people.

→ Write about a time when you were a beginner and learned something new. How did it feel? What did you learn about yourself in the process?

→ Do something today that feels a little bit outside of your comfort zone. Notice how it feels to challenge yourself.

→ Sign up to join a new course, activity, or online community that you're interested in.

Creativity

→ Create a mood board for how you'd like your life to feel. Try to focus on images and words that evoke the feelings you'd like to experience, rather than things you'd like to have.

→ Write about your most joyful memory. What is it about that memory that sparks joy?

→ Plant something. Whether it's a bulb in your garden or some chilli seeds in a pot on your kitchen window, planting something and tending to it can help to instil hope for the future.

→ Identify the most undesirable task on your to-do list today, and then ask yourself, "How can I make this as fun as possible?" Give yourself permission to add a little joy and creativity to even the most mundane or frustrating task.

→ Laugh. Watch some comedy, share an in-joke with a friend, or listen to a funny podcast. Notice how a true belly laugh is good for the soul.

→ Make a note of any quotes or mantras that inspire you to turn to when you need a boost.

→ Get creative with your outfit today and style something differently than how you usually would.

→ Make a joy jar. On some slips of paper, write down activities or things that are guaranteed to bring you joy, fold them up, and put them in a jar. Then, whenever you need a joy boost, take an idea out of the jar.

Gratitude

→ Write a list of ten things you feel grateful for today.

→ Write a list of three things that went well in your life this week. It doesn't matter how big or small. Then, reflect on the role you played in making those things go well.

→ Say a heartfelt thank you to someone you meet today. It doesn't matter who you say it to or what you're thanking them for, but expressing your gratitude has the double benefit of making both you and the recipient feel great!

→ Consider what you have in your life that your grandparents didn't have access to when they were your age. What parts of your everyday life would they have felt most grateful for?

→ Write a letter of gratitude to someone who has had a big impact on your life. You don't have to send it to them, but if you feel comfortable doing so, it can be a powerful way to connect!

→ Cast your mind back to this time last year. What has changed since then that you feel grateful for?

→ Think about a situation you're struggling with. Can you find gratitude for any element of the situation?

→ Tell one of your loved ones about something they do that makes your life better.

→ Write a list of the people in your life you're most grateful for and why.

→ Make a list of three things causing negativity in your life. Then, challenge yourself to see them in a positive light. For example, maybe that leaking roof can be a reminder of how lucky you are to have your own home; the annoying boss could be a reminder of the security your job provides; or the workout you don't want to do could be an opportunity to show thanks for your healthy body.

Bonus

➙ Write a letter from your future self. Picture yourself far in the future— for example, celebrating your ninetieth birthday. Imagine that your life has gone as well as it possibly could have, and you're reflecting on all of the memories you've made, things you've achieved, and lessons you've learned. Then, write a letter from this future you. What advice do they have for the current you?

➙ Look at your schedule for the upcoming week. Add some joy to your calendar.

➙ Choose one of your values and think about an action you can take to feel more aligned to it.

➙ On your phone, create a folder of photos and videos that never fail to make you smile.

➙ Bring some nature indoors by buying yourself some flowers or a plant.

➙ Write down three things you're feeling hopeful about.

➙ Make a list of your top five strengths. How can you use one of them today?

➙ Have a little pamper. Take the time to give yourself a mini facial or manicure.

➙ Pet an animal. Research shows that stroking a cat or dog for ten minutes can reduce your stress levels.

➙ Take a look at your joy wheel. Which area of your life is rated lowest? Think of one thing you can do today to boost the score.

➙ Spend ten minutes visualising the most joyful version of your life. Try to recall all of the little details.

➙ Check in with the goals you set in Chapter Seven. What can you do today to move a little closer to achieving them?

➙ Revisit the list of things that boost your energy from Chapter One. Complete one of the things on the list.

➙ Pick a number from one to ten to sum up how you're feeling today, with ten being as good as can be and one being pretty awful. What is something you could do today to bump the score up by one point?

→ Put just three things on your to-do list today.

→ Think about a decision you're trying to make and use your values to help you explore your options. Which choice aligns best with your values?

CONCLUSION

At the start of this book, I shared a question that I get asked regularly: Why is joy so important? I hope that over the course of the last nine chapters, I've given you the answer.

Joy isn't a reward for hard work, or something we have to earn—it is an essential part of our humanity. It's the stuff of life, something to savour and cherish and cling to, not something to sacrifice or postpone until a later date. Joy is your birthright. You are worthy of it, right here, right now, despite what our capitalistic and patriarchal systems might have tried to convince you. It's yours for the taking, and all you have to do is choose it.

And there is so much of it to go around! There is an abundance of joy to be found in every single day. From the friendly chat with your neighbour, to the unexpected text from a friend. From that first cup of coffee gently sipped in bed, to the cuddles with your pet. From the sound of your kids giggling down the hall, to the pleasure of pulling on your favourite outfit. There is joy to be found in the music you listen to and the books you read and the art you admire. In the stars that unfurl above us every evening, in the sun that rises each day. When you start to look for joy, you can't stop seeing it.

I hope this book has helped you realise that living a joyful life isn't about never feeling sad. It isn't about avoiding the hard parts of life or insuring yourself against negative emotions or experiences. Joy is simply about getting as much value out of the good moments as you can. Life is a swirling mess of joy and grief, of hope and despair, of beauty and terror. Joyful living is about holding as much space for the good as you do the bad. I hope I've given you the tools that help you to do that.

There is never a "perfect time" to start choosing joy. You can't put it off until work settles down, or your kids are a bit older, or you have a little more money in the bank. Any joy you sacrifice now is gone forever, so stop waiting, and start choosing. Seize this moment by taking some action, even the smallest step. You won't regret it.

It has been the biggest pleasure and privilege to write this book for you. Joy has changed my life in ways that I will never stop feeling grateful for, and I know it can do the same for you. I've shared with you everything I know about joy, and now that knowledge is yours to choose what to do with. I hope you choose to build a life for yourself that fills you with love, warmth, and gratitude every day.

For now, let me leave you with some little reminders.

Measure your days not by how much work you have done, but by how much joy you have experienced. Leave work on time, make the most of your lunch breaks, leave tasks on your to-do list unticked—work will wait but your life won't.

Tune into what makes you feel good and do more of it. Don't wait for any-body else to give you permission. Know that your desire is reason enough.

Spend less time seeing life through a screen and more time out there living it. Spend less time watching what everyone else is up to, and more time mak-ing your own stuff happen. Remember that the best way to avoid comparison is to stay committed to living a joyful life.

Notice the stories you're telling about yourself. Question where they came from and discard any that no longer serve you. Strive to make your stories more positive, more generous, and more optimistic.

Practise gratitude at every opportunity. Remember that you really don't need a lot to live a joyful life. Focus on the small everyday glimmers of happiness and don't take any of it for granted.

Tell the people you love how much you love them. Show them, too.

Be open to new opportunities. Adopt an attitude of curiosity and flexibility, instead of trying to plan every moment. Sometimes the very best memories are made when you least expect them. Know that feeling scared is okay every now and then, so long as it's moving you in the right direction.

Keep on learning. Give yourself permission to change your mind often—the smartest people usually do. Read books, listen to music, have interesting con-versations. Notice what captures your curiosity and give yourself some space to explore it. You never know where that curiosity will lead.

Don't fall into the trap of trying to shrink yourself to fit in. Instead, strive to take up more space. Add more beauty to your life instead of stripping things away. Use joy as your North Star instead of willpower or expectation. Notice how it helps you to sleep better at night.

Look up at the stars often and remember how insignificant we all are. Look around at your loved ones often and remember how important you are to them.

Spend more time outdoors. Swim in the sea, walk on the moors, get lost in the woods. Stretch. Get up early to watch the sunrise; stay up late to watch the sunset. Take time to notice the seasons changing around you.

Keep checking in with yourself. Journal or meditate if you can. Work on building a relationship with your intuition. Listen to your gut—it's usually right.

Look for the good, especially when times get tricky. Even during the toughest periods, there are always people helping, and there is always good to be found. Focusing on it will make you feel less alone.

And finally, know that you are worthy. Of the joy, of the love, of the warmth. Of the opportunities, of the ease, of the beauty. Choosing joy for yourself is a radical act—embrace it. I will be rooting for you every single step of the way.

JOYFUL RESOURCES

If you're looking for some further resources to help you navigate your joy journey, I've got you covered. Here are some of my favourite books and podcasts.

Books

Burnout: The Secret to Unlocking the Stress Cycle By Emily Nagoski, PhD and Amelia Nagoski, DMA

This book is a game changer when it comes to stress and burnout, blending interesting and ground-breaking research with a witty, real-world approach to help you tackle overwhelm and exhaustion.

Write Yourself Happy: The Art of Positive Journalling by Megan C. Hayes, PhD

If you'd like to try journalling more often, I couldn't recommend this brilliant book more. Hayes shares some interesting research on the power of positive journalling, as well as plenty of prompts to get you started.

Untamed by Glennon Doyle

If you need a reminder that joy is your birthright and a confidence boost to reject the expectations society places upon us, this is the book for you. Its unique blend of memoir and rallying cry makes it a real page-turner, and I recommend it to just about everyone I meet!

How to be Hopeful: Your Toolkit to Rediscover Hope and Help Create a Kinder World by Bernadette Russell

Hope is an essential part of building a joyful life, and this book shares some practical wisdom on how to cultivate more of it in your life.

The Joy of Small Things by Hannah Jane Parkinson

A collection of essays on the joy of small things, this book serves as a brilliant reminder of the power of feeling grateful for all of the everyday joys available to us.

Year of Yes: How to Dance It Out, Stand in the Sun and Be Your Own Person by Shonda Rhimes

Written by prolific writer, executive producer, and showrunner Shonda Rhimes, this book is a moving and beautiful reminder of what lies on the other side of the changes we desire and how things can improve when we just start saying YES.

Daring Greatly: How the Courage to Be Vulnerable Transforms the Way We Live, Love, Parent, and Lead by Brené Brown

Brené Brown is one of my all-time icons, and this book truly changed my life. It explores the power of vulnerability in helping us to build more authentic and joyful lives and inspires so much courage.

Big Dreams, Daily Joys by Elise Blaha Cripe

This book is basically one big permission slip to set goals that feel truly joyful to you. It also provides further inspiration on how to stay motivated to achieve those goals.

Playing Big: Practical Wisdom for Women Who Want to Speak Up, Create, and Lead by Tara Mohr

If you need a reminder of your potential, this book is the one for you. Tara Mohr does a fantastic job of helping you to see why you're already good enough for the life and career of your dreams. This book is like rocket fuel for your confidence.

Podcasts

The Happiness Lab with Dr. Laurie Santos

Dr. Laurie Santos leads the most popular class at Yale—Psychology and the Good Life—where she teaches on the science of well-being. In this illuminating podcast, she shares many of those teachings and conducts thought-provoking interviews that are both inspiring and research-led.

We Can Do Hard Things with Glennon Doyle

As we've talked about in this book, making any sort of change is hard. In this podcast, Glennon Doyle, along with her sister and wife, is on hand to remind you that you can do hard things. Listening to this podcast is like having a cheerleader in your pocket—someone who believes in you unconditionally and will gently coach you to keep getting back up and trying again.

Happy Place with Fearne Cotton

As we've discussed in this book, joy and happiness look different for all of us. Fearne Cotton explores these complexities on the *Happy Place* podcast with her guests, who include everyone from Deepak Chopra to Alicia Keys.

Unlocking Us with Brené Brown

Brené Brown's podcast, *Unlocking Us*, is jam-packed full of inspiring conversations on all things emotion, meaning, and connection. I always leave every episode with a new idea or tip to put into action.

Happier with Gretchen Rubin

When it comes to happiness, what are the practical tips, hacks, and ideas that can help us? That's exactly what Gretchen Rubin and her co-host, Elizabeth Craft, discuss in their podcast, *Happier*. If you're looking for some small, practical actions you can take along your joy journey, this is the one for you.

ACKNOWLEDGEMENTS

After spending so much of this book waxing lyrical about the power of gratitude, it feels pretty special to end it by sharing some heartfelt thank yous of my own.

Before I started working on this book, I was completely naive to what a huge undertaking it would be. I am so grateful to the team at Blue Star Press for all of their hard work at every stage, and for making this project a true joy to work on together.

Particular thanks to my editorial director, Lindsay Wilkes-Edrington, not only for trusting me with this book, but also for being so generous with your knowledge, patience, and insight as we turned those initial ideas into something real. Writing a book is no easy feat, but your feedback and enthusiasm gave me confidence when I needed it most!

Thank you to all of the clients and students who have trusted me to walk alongside them on their own joy journey over the years. I get to do the work I love every day because of you, and that feels like the greatest privilege.

Thank you to Kris Kelly and Vicky Kelly, both for allowing me to write about Blossom, and also for being the very best examples of continuing to choose joy even when life deals you the most difficult hand. Your strength and courage never fail to inspire me.

To my very own girl gang—Emily, Fiona, Steph, Spils, Sarah, Teddy, and Jess—thank you for being by my side for all of the highs and lows of the last decade and a half, and for always cheering me on with love and good humour. Extra special thanks to Fiona and Emily for keeping me sane during the writing process and putting up with all of the terrible selfies of me with unwashed hair in my pyjamas whenever I was on a deadline.

To Lyla and Ralf, being your Auntie Sophie is my greatest joy. Thank you for expanding my heart ten times over and for reminding me that there's always time for one more push on the swings, one more story, one more cuddle. Thank you to Darcey, Honey, Hudson, Buddy, and all of the other wonderful kids I'm lucky enough to have in my life. Playing even the smallest role in your childhood makes me feel so proud.

To Mum and Dad, I could fill a whole book with the thank yous I owe you. I don't take either of you for granted. The older I get, the more I realise what a privilege your unconditional love and unwavering pride in me really is. To my sister, Molly, thank you for always keeping me grounded and for being the funniest person I know. You don't know how lucky I feel to have a built-in best friend.

And finally, to my ever-patient husband, Sam. Without you, there's no book, no business, no joy. Thank you for keeping me fed and watered, for taking on more than your fair share, and for always being there to celebrate the big and small wins. You are a true partner in every sense of the word, and I will never stop feeling grateful for you.

NOTES

Introduction

Park, Nansook, Christopher Peterson, Daniel Szvarca, Randy J. Vander Molen, Eric S. Kim, and Kevin Collon. 2016. "Positive Psychology and Physical Health." *American Journal of Lifestyle Medicine* Vol. 10 (3): 200-06: https://www.ncbi.nlm.nih.gov/pmc/articles/PMC6124958/.

Lyubomirsky, Sonja and Laura King. 2005. "The Benefits of Frequent Positive Affect: Does Happiness Lead to Success?" *Psychological Bulletin* Vol. 131 (6): 803-55. https://escholarship.org/content/qt1k08m32k/qt1k-08m32k.pdf.

Chapter 1

Fredrickson, Barbara L. 2004. "The Broaden-and-Build Theory of Positive Emotions." The Royal Society. https://www.ncbi.nlm.nih.gov/pmc/articles/PMC1693418/pdf/15347528.pdf.

Mental Health Foundation. 2018. "Stressed Nation: 74% of UK Overwhelmed or Unable to Cope' at Some Point in the Past Year." Mentalhealth.org. https://www.mentalhealth.org.uk/news/stressed-nation-74-uk-overwhelmed-or-unable-cope-some-point-past-year.

Chapter 2

Ryan, Richard M. and Edward L. Deci. 2000. "Intrinsic and Extrinsic Motivations: Classic Definitions and New Directions." Contemporary Educational Psychology Vol. 25: 54-67. https://selfdeterminationtheory.org/SDT/documents/2000_RyanDeci_IntExtDefs.pdf.

Chapter 4

Conner, Tamlin S., Colin G. DeYoung, and Paul J. Silvia. 2016. "Everyday Creativity as a Path to Joy." *The Journal of Positive Psychology* Vol. 13 (2): 181-89. https://doi.org/10.1080/17439760.2016.1257049.

Hendriks, Tom, Meg A. Warren, Marijke Schotanus-Dijkstra, Aabidien Hassankhan, Tobi Graafsman, Ernst Bohlmeijer, and Joop de Jong. 2018. "How WEIRD are Positive Psychology Interventions? A Bibliometric Analysis of Randomized Controlled Trials on the Science of Well-Being." *The Journal of Positive Psychology* Vol. 14 (4): 489-501. https://www.tandfonline.com/doi/abs/10.1080/17439760.2018.1484941.

Huppert, Felicia A., Nick Baylis, and Barry Keverne. 2005. "Physically Active Lifestyles and Well-Being." *The Science of Well-Being* published to Oxford Scholarship Online, accessed June 23, 2022. https://doi.org/10.1093/acprof:oso/9780198567523.003.0006.

Kennelly, Stacey. 2012. "10 Steps to Savoring the Good Things in Life." *Greater Good Magazine*, July 23, 2012. https://greatergood.berkeley.edu/article/item/10_steps_to_savoring_the_good_things_in_life.

King, Laura A. 2001. "The Health Benefits of Writing about Life Goals." *Personality and Social Psychology Bulletin* Vol. 27 (7): 798–807. https://doi.org/10.1177/0146167201277003.

Lyubomirsky, Sonja and Laura King. 2005. "The Benefits of Frequent Positive Affect: Does Happiness Lead to Success?" *Psychological Bulletin* Vol. 131 (6): 803-55. https://escholarship.org/content/qt1k08m32k/qt1k-08m32k.pdf.

Mineo, Liz. 2017. "Good Genes are Nice, but Joy is Better." *The Harvard Gazette*, April 11, 2017. https://news.harvard.edu/gazette/story/2017/04/over-nearly-80-years-harvard-study-has-been-showing-how-to-live-a-healthy-and-happy-life/.

University of Texas at Austin. 2020. "Spending on Experiences Versus Possessions Advances More Immediate Happiness." ScienceDaily. Last modified March 9, 2020. https://www.sciencedaily.com/releases/2020/03/200309130020.htm.

Chapter 5

Brené Brown on joy and gratitude, Global Leadership Network. https://globalleadership.org/articles/leading-yourself/ brene-brown-on-joy-and-gratitude/.

Brown, Brené. 2018. "Brené Brown on Joy and Gratitude." Global Leadership Network, November 21, 2018. https://globalleadership.org/articles/ leading-yourself/brene-brown-on-joy-and-gratitude/.

Sansone, R.A. and L.A. Sansone. 2010. "Gratitude and Well Being: the Benefits of Appreciation." Psychiatry Vol. 7 (11): 18-21. https://psycnet.apa. org/record/2010-25532-003.

Chapter 6

John Templeton Foundation. 2018. "The Psychology of Purpose." Accessed June 23, 2022. https://www.templeton.org/discoveries/ the-psychology-of-purpose.

Greater Good Magazine. n.d. "What is Purpose?" Accessed June 20, 2022. https://greatergood.berkeley.edu/topic/purpose/definition.

Kang, Yoona, Danielle Cosme, Rui Rei, Prateekshit Pandey, José Carreras-Tartak, and Emily B. Falk. 2021. "Purpose in Life, Loneliness, and Protective Health Behaviors During the COVID-19 Pandemic." The Gerontologist Vol. 61 (6): 878-87. https://doi.org/10.1093/geront/gnab081.

Chapter 7

Boniwell, Ilona, and Aneta D. Tunariu. 2019. Positive Psychology: Theory, Research and Applications. 2nd ed. London: Open University Press. Chapter 7: 159.

Gardner, Sarah and Dave Albee. 2015. "Study Focuses on Strategies for Achieving Goals, Resolutions." Dominican University of California Press Release, February 1, 2015. https://scholar.dominican.edu/news-releases/266.

ABOUT THE AUTHOR

Sophie Cliff (aka The Joyful Coach) is a qualified coach and positive psychology practitioner. Sophie holds an MSc in Applied Positive Psychology and Coaching Psychology from the University of East London. She has supported hundreds of clients in making joyful changes in their lives. In 2021, she founded Joy Futures, a workplace well-being consultancy designed to help organisations bring the joy back to work. She is also the host of chart-topping podcast *Practical Positivity*.

Sophie lives in Leeds, United Kingdom, with her husband, Sam, and their cat, Lola. She finds joy in long walks in the countryside, time spent with her family, and reading brilliant books.